NATIVE AMERICANS ON FILM AND VIDEO

VOLUME II

ELIZABETH WEATHERFORD AND EMELIA SEUBERT

MUSEUM OF THE AMERICAN INDIAN/HEYE FOUNDATION

© 1988 Museum of the American Indian
Broadway at 155th Street, New York, New York 10032
ISBN 0-934490-44-9
Library of Congress Catalog Card No. 81-85266
Printed by Capital City Press, Montpelier, Vermont

Native Americans on Film and Video has received major funding from the New York
State Council on the Arts and the National Endowment for the Arts.

CONTENTS

INTRODUCTION

Since the publication in 1981 of the first volume of NATIVE AMERICANS ON FILM AND VIDEO, the Film and Video Center of the Museum of the American Indian has been established as a national media center and information service concerned with films and videotapes about native peoples of North, Central, South America, and the Arctic. Through its exhibitions and services the Center provides assistance to a large public, including film- and videomakers, programmers, museum and community media organizations, researchers, television producers, educators, and tribal communities and organizations.

NATIVE AMERICANS ON FILM AND VIDEO, VOLUME II, provides information on approximately 200 productions, selected from works made since 1980. Many of these have been exhibited by the Film and Video Center in its Native American Film and Video Festival and other screenings. Most works described are documentaries, with short fictional films and animations included, and most have been produced by independent media makers. They reflect a diversity of viewpoints, styles, and production values. The selections have been made on the basis of the quality of the productions' research, filming, and editing, and on the uniqueness of their approach or subject matter, including profiles of native groups about whom few films have been available. Many works by Native American independent producers, native media centers, or tribal communities working in cooperation with independent media makers have been included (see Native American media categories in the Subjects index).

Although the catalog entries attempt to describe the works fully, it is essential for users of any production listed to view it before screening it for their audiences. The productions vary in focus; some stress traditional ways, others concentrate on contemporary issues facing Native Americans. In addition, the technical quality of the productions varies. The skillful programmer will wish to take this into consideration in deciding which works to screen.

The contents of this catalog are the responsibility of its authors, Elizabeth Weatherford, Associate Curator, and Emelia Seubert, Assistant Curator, of the Film and Video Center of the Museum of the American Indian. Project assistants during its preparation have been Katherine Renner Pourshariati, Gray Hollett, and Judy White Feather.

HOW TO USE THE CATALOG

The listings, arrange alphabetically, include descriptions of individual productions, important series, and production groups. Works from the same production group often are listed under the description of the group. Information given on each film or videotape includes:

 –release date
 –running time (to the nearest minute)

-production credits (producer, director, camera, sound, and other significant personnel)

-formats available (film: 35mm or 16mm; videotape: ¾" NCTS, ½" VHS, ½" Betamax. "All video formats" indicates 1" videotape is also available)

-languages (other than English) either spoken in the work or in which the production is available

-distributors for both sales and rentals (unless otherwise specified)

Indexes by subject and by tribe and region are included for ease in locating titles. An up-to-date distributors' list for both VOLUMES I and II is also included.

FILMSTRIPS AND SLIDE TAPES

For users of film strips and slide tapes, a separate listing of recommended productions has been compiled by Yvonne Beamer, New York State Native American Education Program. To obtain a copy send a stamped, self-addressed envelope to FVC-MAI (see distributor's index).

ACKNOWLEDGEMENTS

We are grateful for the invaluable assistance of Malcolm Arth and Nathaniel Johnson, American Museum of Natural History, New York City; Yvonne Beamer, New York State Native American Education Program, New York City; Brian Camp, CUNY-TV, New York City; Mary Davis, Museum of the American Indian Library; George Eager, New York City; G. Peter Jemison, Ganondagan State Historic Site, Victor, New York; Joel Kanoff, Educational Film Library Association, New York City; Mary Jane Lenz, Museum of the American Indian; Huguette Parent, National Film Board of Canada, Montreal; James G. E. Smith, Museum of the American Indian; Pierre Stevens, Moving Image and Sound Archives, Public Archives of Canada, Ottawa; Florence Stone, Earthwatch, Washington, D.C.; Robert Summers, Film/Audio Services, New York City; and the many film- and videomakers and distributors whose productions we have had the privilege of viewing and exhibiting. Finally, we wish to thank Dr. Roland W. Force, President and Director of the Museum of the American Indian.

CURRENTS
FILM AND VIDEO IN NATIVE AMERICA

Since the beginning of filmmaking, Native Americans have been the subject of virtually thousands of works by both Hollywood directors and documentary producers. Not until the 1970's, with the rise of independent film and video, did native perspectives begin to be reflected. Production by Native Americans began in a period of intense Indian political activism. The takeovers at Wounded Knee and Alcatraz Island dramatized native peoples' rights and their oppression to an entire world. In the politically liberalized climate of the era, greater control of their own lives seemed possible. Conscious of the power of media, Native Americans began to actively participate in productions about their traditions and viewpoints, as on-camera subjects, as co-producers, and as independent producers themselves.

During these years the governments of both Canada and the United States felt obligated to assist ethnic minorities, including Native Americans, in educational and cultural spheres. Training and employment in radio and television became more available, and independent film projects were funded to articulate native views. In Canada, the National Film Board trained producers and completed documentary films in its "Challenge for Change" program. In most provinces and territories, financial assistance was offered to help form native communications societies, now with a national headquarters in Ottawa. In the late 1970's a pilot television experiment led to the formation of the Inuit Broadcasting Corporation. It produces programs in the Inuktitut language in different Arctic communities and airs them via satellite across the region.

In the United States, national and state funding became available for developing Native American educational materials, emphasizing tribal involvement. Film and video series from various regions were made, including areas where tribes' histories were little known to the general public — for example, southern New England (*People of the First Light*) and the Plateau (*The Real People*). Some tribes produced works for early childhood education (the Seneca Nation's *Keeper of the Western Door*).

During this decade Indian media makers met with representatives of national public television and formed the Native American Public Broadcasting Consortium to provide programs about native people to television stations in the United States. Unfortunately few Native American productions have been aired nationally. In addition, no national system has been created to target support for the training of native media makers or specifically to fund native productions.

Some tribes are moving against this tide by producing videotapes for use in their own communities. Tribal media productions record local events and conserve the knowledge and skills of elders. Pioneering the establishment of media departments, through the initiative of committed individuals and often despite limited funding, are such tribes as the Muscogee Creek Nation (Oklahoma) and the Ute Indian Tribe (Utah). Now telecommunications alternatives — low-power and cable broadcast systems — can offer wider public access of tribally-produced works as well.

The exhibition of films and videotapes in other contexts — festivals, cinema-theques, and museums — has also expanded. Since the mid-1970's the American Indian Film Festival in San Francisco and the Native American Film and Video Festival in New York City have screened outstanding new works. Through information and exhibition services, including a traveling film festival, *Native America Now*, the Museum of the American Indian's Film and Video Center is bringing recent productions by independents and Native American media makers into a wider arena.

In recent years Latin America has also been developing both independent media and Indian community video. Since 1985 the Festival Latinoamericano de Cine de Pueblas Indigenas has screened works on Indians of the region. Support for native videomaking is increasing, a notable example being a collaboration in production and training between Kayapo Indians and an independent video group in Brazil.

Today Native American film- and videomakers' work reflects many impulses — to combat stereotypes, to address an information gap in non-native society, and to reinforce the cultural heritage of the community. Because of the pressures to assimilate which they have experienced, Native Americans' productions on cultural revival and traditions have a political dimension not usually associated with this kind of documentary. Works by these producers also directly address political issues, focusing on central concerns such as land rights and sovereignty. In some of the most recent Native American films and videotapes the possibility of new aesthetics, expressive of Indian and Inuit frameworks, are also being explored by reaching inward to native oral and visual traditions.

FILM AND VIDEO LISTINGS

ABNAKI: THE NATIVE PEOPLE OF MAINE

1982, 28 min. Producer/director/writer: Jay Kent. Editor: Michel Chalufour. Produced for the Maine Tribal Governors, Inc. 16mm, ¾" vt. Color. Dist.: Barr/Centre.

The land claims suit of the Passamaquoddy and Penobscot tribes of Maine, which received much press attention in the late 1970's, was highly influential for other Indian groups in the United States. Life for people of these and other Maine tribes is documented in ABNAKI whose title refers to the confederacy of Algonkian-speaking tribes forged hundreds of years ago in this region. The film was shot near Passamaquoddy Bay in southeast Maine and at the Penboscot reservation near Old Town in northern Maine. Tribal leaders cooperated in the making of the film and tribal members participated as production crew and advisors.

Although initially disregarded by the state legislature, which has formal governmental relations with the tribes, their claims have been proven legitimate. In 1980 the case was settled out of court, with money offered to the tribes to purchase back lands to which they are entitled. As briefly mentioned in the film, the Malecite and Micmac tribes continue to have claims not settled in this case.

Speaking on-camera, members of the tribes discuss issues, from educational systems hostile to Indian culture to tourism. Living on the Atlantic seaboard, their people's exposure to white culture began over 350 years ago, radically affecting native languages, religious practices, traditional economies, and land uses. One effect of this is that most Americans, thinking Indians live only in the West, know little about the Maine tribes. These people's expressions of concern about acculturation and the survival of Indian values, however, echo Native American experiences throughout the continent.

Vignettes of contemporary Indian life include a storyteller spinning a yarn and discussion of the loss or preservation of the native language. People express concern that their way of life, characterized by sharing and community loyalty, be sustained in the face of the white economy. Hopes for the future are expressed eloquently by Penobscot leader Eunice Nelson. "We have survived poverty, oppression, racism, dissension. This has made me wonder how we survived. Because of traditional Indian beliefs that have persisted, we have had the strength."

ALASKA NATIVE CLAIMS SETTLEMENT ACT

For description see *Northwest Arctic Video.*

ALASKA: THE YUP'IK ESKIMOS

1985, 27 min. Co-producer/director: Larry Lansburgh. Co-producer/writer: Gail Evanari. Camera: Randy Love. Sound: Jim Manson. Editor: Jennifer Gallagher. Produced by Chevron U.S.A. Executive producer: Susan Duncan. ½" vt. Color. Dist.: Chevron (free loan).

ALASKA: THE YUP'IK ESKIMOS focuses on changes in Yup'ik culture and way of life, with commentary provided by people from four communities — Bethel, Eek, Chevak, and Tooksook Bay. As elders discuss the continuing importance of the land as the basis for subsistence, the film juxtaposes contemporary hunting scenes with historical footage. Traditional native foods remain a central expression of Yup'ik culture. Scenes show a family at its summer camp site, where men and boys fish with nets, women process and preserve fish, and the children gather berries. At a gathering at a village community center, the people feast on traditional foods, and their dances celebrate the hunting way of life.

The film also depicts changes in village life — children play basketball, dance at a disco, and learn to use computers. The difficulties faced by the young in balancing the old and the new are mentioned by both elders and young people. Elders are a valued source of knowledge of traditions, and their important role in cultural continuity is beautifully illustrated in scenes of a man teaching his grandson dance movements.

Produced through a corporate educational media program, this filmed overview of Yup'ik culture today is designed for use in grades 7–12, but it is very suitable for adult audiences. A study guide in English or Yup'ik is available, but must be requested separately from the production (see distributors index).

ALPACA BREEDERS OF CHIMBOYA

1984, 30 min. Director: Marianne Eyde. Produced by Kusi Films. 16mm, ¾" vt, ½" vt. Color. In Spanish or English. Dist.: Icarus.

This ethnographic film documents the life of a small Indian peasant community in the region of Puno in the Andean highlands of Peru where the marketing of alpaca fleece is essential to survival. All aspects of the people's economic life, from the rituals related to shearing the alpaca to marketing and bartering activities, are depicted, providing a context for understanding the villagers' way of life.

Eighty-five percent of Peruvian alpaca wool is exported, and the textile export companies' profits depend on their ability to control prices. Their buyers extend credit, building permanent indebtedness into the peasants' lives. The peasants are also tied to the middlemen through godfather arrangements and feel a moral obligation to sell to "their" company. The film shows that when cash runs low during the year, however, the Indians of different communities survive by bartering among themselves.

ALPACA BREEDERS OF CHIMBOYA offers a clear example of how Indian peasants in South America provide products which serve as commodities in the world economic system. It illustrates how profitability for the companies and the economic stability of such nations as Peru depend on exploiting these village producers. The film concludes by suggesting that a solution will be found only when the Indians establish greater control over the marketing system for their products.

AN ANCIENT GIFT

1982, 18 min. Producer/writers: Donald Coughlin and Therese Burson. Director: Donald Coughlin. Camera: Randy Love. Sound: Nelson Stoll. Produced for the Museum of Northern Arizona, Flagstaff. Project director: Robert J. Breunig. 16mm, ¾" vt. Color. In English or Navajo. Dist.: UCEMC.

"To care for sheep like a mother is, for the Navajo, to care for the Navajo people."

The central role that sheep herds traditionally play in Navajo life is the focus of this film. Scenes from daily activities are intercut with shots of the Navajo homeland in Arizona, showing the interdependence of the people, their land, and their flocks. Young children are shown tending herds. A mother and her daughter-in-law card, spin, and dye wool before weaving it. A father butchers a sheep for the meat and hide it will provide for the family's use.

The importance of their flocks to the Navajo is highlighted not only by the demonstration of how products from the sheep are made and used, but also by reference to the Navajo belief that sheep originated as an ancient gift from Changing Woman. By focusing on subsistence and showing this key aspect of Navajo life in mythic and in practical terms, the film provides an excellent short introduction to Navajo traditional culture. It is one of two films produced by Coughlin for the Museum of Northern Arizona to contextualize its exhibitions on Navajo and Hopi cultures (see description of CORN IS LIFE in this volume).

ANCIENT SPIRIT, LIVING WORD
For description see *Through This Darkest Night*.

ANGOON-100 YEARS LATER
1983, 30 min. Producer/director/writer: Laurence Goldin. Produced for the Kootznoowoo Heritage Foundation at KTOO-TV, Anchorage, AK. Executive producer: G. Eve Reckley. ¾" vt. Color. Dist.: Aurora.

Through interviews, old photographs, and the filming of an emotionally charged ceremony, this videotape presents the people and history of the Tlingit community of Angoon, Alaska. Aspects of ceremony are discussed, to explain to the viewer their value to the community. For example, the tape opens with shots of the ceremonial warming of hands and states that new and old ceremonial objects and clothing are being worn and used. The older pieces have greater emotional value to the clan, the explanation continues, because they have come to embody the people who wore them before.

The occasion for the potlatch is multiple. Those assembled have come to witness the formal giving of clan names to young people, as well as to the former Alaska governor Osmund Hammond, and are also honoring elder Jimmy George. But the event that is being commemorated is the hundredth anniversary of an attack against Angoon, on October 26, 1882, in which gunships of the United States Navy destroyed the village. The background for this event is told with emphasis on the consistent misunderstanding and denigration of the Tlingits during the late nineteenth century, as well as the suffering caused by the village's destruction. The community has requested an official apology, but during the ceremony there are two minutes of silence in observation of the fact that it has never been given.

ANGOON provides information about the traditional structure of Tlingit clan and family relations and the place of the potlatch as a multi-dimensional event which explores history, observes traditional ways, and celebrates the culture's continuity. In addition, it shows the kind of events in the history of Native American communities that have shaped their understanding of the white world.

ANIMATIONS AT CAPE DORSET
For description see *Magic in the Sky*.

ANOTHER WIND IS MOVING

For description see *Return to Sovereignty.*

APACHE MOUNTAIN SPIRITS

1985, 58 min. Producer: John H. Crouch. Director: Bob Graham. Associate producer: Jennie D. Crouch. Associate director/stage manager: Kate Quillan-Graham. Screenplay: Joy Harjo and Henry Greenberg. Director of photography: Russ Carpenter. Consultant: Edgar Perry. Produced for the White Mountain Apache Tribe. ¾" vt, ½" vt. Color. In English and Apache with English subtitles. Dist.: Silvercloud.

An explanation of the role of the *Gaan*, the Mountain Spirits who are the source of sacred power for the Apache, is told through two stories, set in ancient and modern times, in a production sponsored by the White Mountain Apache Tribe. The actors, who are tribe members, play comparable parts in both stories. In the ancient time a young boy receives power in dreams that lead to his joining the Gaan. Through him his people learn the Crown Dance, whose performance is central to Apache religious ceremonies. This story appears to the present-day Apache boy as a series of dreams.

In the contemporary story Robert, a boarding school runaway, returns home. His uncle counsels him to remember that the Apache respect wisdom revealed in dreams, and that dreamers have a responsibility for using the power they receive for good or evil. The boy is persuaded by a companion to join in a house break-in. At the last moment, refusing to participate, he is seriously wounded. At the same time in the ancient story a climactic scene takes place in which the people meet with the Gaan and join them in the dance which is the origin of the Crown Dance. The ancient story closes with the boy leaving with the Gaan; Robert recovers, having gained new wisdom from his experience.

The integration of the two stories is well conceived, achieving with clarity the production's goal of showing the relevance of ancient Apache ways for today's young people. As a project made in close cooperation with tribal consultants who provided and shaped the content, much of which is of a sacred nature, APACHE MOUNTAIN SPIRITS has an authenticity rare in dramatic re-enactments of tribal culture.

ARCTIC SPIRITS

1983, 27 min. Producers: Katherine Marielle and Peter Raymont. Director/writer: Peter Raymont. Camera: Martin Duckworth. Sound: Claude Beaugrant. Editor: Barry Greenwald. Narrator: Roy Bonisteel. Consultant: Asen Balikci. Produced for the Canadian Broadcasting Corporation series Man Alive. *16mm, ¾" vt. Color. Dist.: Investigative.*

An investigation of the rise of evangelical Christianity in Inuit villages in the Canadian Arctic, this documentary interviews both participants and observers of this religious movement and testifies to the far-reaching impact in the North of television and other aspects of Canadian culture. It touches upon the complex issue of how contemporary Inuit are meeting their needs for spiritual and material survival today.

In exploring the impact of events of the past century on Inuit spiritual expression, the film discusses the traditional shamans, known as *angakuk*, and their practices. Footage of a healing ceremony, shot in 1961 as part of a film project in which Netsilikimiut re-enacted ancient Inuit activities, and a short animation by a young Inuit to evoke angakuk spiritual flight, are exceptionally interesting. In an interview, anthropologist Asen Balikci suggests that evangelical practices, such as healing by touch, may be culturally acceptable to some Inuit because of their apparent similarities to ancient religious ways.

The film follows three Canadian evangelists on their crusades in Arctic Quebec and the Northwest Territories. During the services Inuit believers are seen to speak in tongues and be "slain in the spirit." Some Inuit Christians describe how their religion provides an alternative to a life overwhelmed by alcohol or drugs, or by problems stemming from the massive unemployment typical of the region.

The film also interviews Inuit who describe the evangelical movement as exploitative and part of a continuing cultural transformation stimulated by non-Inuit. For example, John Amagoalik, the president of the Inuit Tapirisat, perceives the evangelical movement as in direct conflict with contemporary Inuits' needs to maintain their own way of life and sovereignty. Others criticize it for fostering apathy toward the future. By representing various opposing views voiced by Inuit and non-Inuit, the film shows the complexity of contemporary changes in the life of people of the Arctic.

AYMARA LEADERSHIP

1973/1985, 29 min. Producer: Norman Miller. Director/sound: Hubert Smith. Camera: Neil Reichline. Editor: Michael Akestar. Advisors: Dwight Heath and A.C. Heath. Produced with the collaboration of the Universities Field Staff. ¾" vt. Color. In Aymara with English subtitles. Dist.: Smith.

This innovative videotape studies leadership and conflict resolution in an Aymara community in the Bolivian Andes. Filmed in the village of Vitocota, it focuses on the village leader, Manuel Ticona, who is Central Secretary of the Agriculture League. (Since land reform in Bolivia, the Agriculture League leaders have largely replaced hereditary leaders.) Ticona's decisions are accepted by the villagers because he satisfies traditional criteria; he observes proper customs, listens to all parties, and actively participates in the solutions which he himself has suggested. Through the use of slow motion, the production shows how Ticona's leadership is expressed through body movement, for example as he stops the progress of a disagreement with a decisive gesture of his arm.

In a single afternoon Ticona sees a number of people in the courtyard of his home, advising on many questions and settling several disputes. He resolves a disagreement between individuals who have quarreled during a recent fiesta and decides what to do with two national identity cards that have been found. In a third case he agrees to endorse the efforts of a man to collect debts on notes that were destroyed in a fire, and convinces the skeptical villagers to help this man by voluntarily paying him what they owe.

In an extended sequence, Ticona accompanies Don Tomas who rents costumes and banners to the villagers for use during the fiesta. He enlists the aid of the *jilikata*, the hereditary village leader, who functions as a witness and symbolically lends authority to the proceedings. At the home of Don Roberto, ritual hospitality precedes the discussion of how the rent, now overdue, will be paid to Don Tomas. The production breaks down the event into a number of stages, showing the negotiations, both parties making concessions, the resolution of the case, and personal interactions that heal the breach in harmony which has occurred. All steps are under the able guidance of Ticona.

Smith is an outstanding visual anthropologist. Here he has taken footage he shot more than ten years ago and, using slow motion, instant replay, and frame-freezing, has effectively shown the subtle aspects of communication that underpin leadership. With intimacy and insight he has documented aspects of Aymara village life that have rarely been filmed. The production's presentation of the villagers' speech through colloquial translation and innovative subtitling and the use of brief title cards for background information adds to the viewer's sense of directly observing events, and understanding them as they happen. For descriptions of other productions by Smith see FACES OF CHANGE SERIES, p. 44–45, and THE MAYA OF CONTEMPORARY YUCATAN (THE LIVING MAYA), p. 76–77, in Volume I, and FACES OF CULTURE SERIES in this volume.

BEAVERTAIL SNOWSHOES
For description see *Trust for Native American Cultures and Crafts Video.*

BOX OF TREASURES
1983, 18 min. Director: Chuck Olin. Camera: Chuck Olin and Tony Westman. Sound: John Mason and David Rosen. Editors: Jill Singer and John Mason. Produced by the U'mista Cultural Society and Chuck Olin Associates. Executive producer: Gloria Cranmer Webster. 16mm, ¾" vt, ½" vt. Color. Dist.: DER (US)/CFDW (Canada).

In 1921 the Canadian government seized from the Kwakiutl numerous ritual objects being used for the performance of a potlatch, a traditional ceremony banned by the government since 1884. In 1980, at Alert Bay, approximately 180 miles north of Vancouver, British Columbia, the U'mista Cultural Centre opened to receive and house the cultural treasures which were returned after years of effort by leading community members (*u'mista* means "the return of something important"). BOX OF TREASURES celebrates the recovery of the objects and documents efforts now underway to revive the cultural heritage diminished during years of suppression and intervention by religious and government organizations. The film's title comes from a statement of one of the elders who sees the Cultural Centre as being like the traditional Kwakiutl storage boxes in which ceremonial objects were kept.

The film shows the Kwakiutl utilizing many resources to facilitate cultural revival and preservation. For example, a linguist works with a Kwakwala speaker to prepare language curriculum materials. Oral histories are recorded on videotape inside the Centre. Children are taught aspects of the culture, from traditional tales to the performance of the majestic dances performed at potlatches. A determined effort by a tribal community ultimately results in greater control of its own future and the continuation of its traditional values.

Throughout the film, Gloria Cranmer Webster, director of the U'mista Cultural Society, speaks eloquently about the way the continuation of culture sustains a people. She sees the current efforts as part of a larger struggle for the right of the Kwakiutl to maintain their culture and their sovereignty. This is the second film produced by the U'mista Cultural Society. In POTLATCH: A STRICT LAW BIDS US DANCE (for description see Volume I, p. 95),

Kwakiutl community members re-enact the events surrounding the seizure of their ceremonial items in 1921.

BROKEN RAINBOW

1985, 70 min. Producer/writer/editors: Maria Florio and Victoria Mudd. Director: Victoria Mudd. Camera: Michael Anderson and Fred Elmes. Sound: Susumu Tukunow and Jim Rosselini. Music: Laura Nyro. Narrator: Martin Sheen. 16mm, ½" vt (sales and rentals), ¾" vt (sales only). Color. Dist.: Direct Cinema.

A forceful film concerned with the relocation of traditional Navajo from their homes in Big Mountain, Arizona, BROKEN RAINBOW won the Academy Award for best documentary in 1985. It provides a sympathetic view of the Navajo perspective on the history of the lands in dispute, and not only clarifies the issue of relocation and protests the policy decisions leading to it, but also serves as an indictment of federal government interference and its power over Indian issues.

The film is strongest in its portrayal of those who are directly affected by relocation, showing traditional Navajos like Catherine Smith at home and in the unfamiliar environment of California where they have traveled to make their plight more visible. It treats only briefly the fact that the lands in question are officially part of the small Hopi reservation. Hopi are affected, though differently, by this situation, but only Hopis who favor the Navajos remaining, most notably the elder Thomas Banyacya, are interviewed.

BROKEN RAINBOW is rooted in the history of the Navajo, who in the 1860's found themselves forcibly acculturated to white ways and placed on a reservation. Hopi-Navajo borders were not always clearly defined, with some Navajos living in traditionally Hopi land, such as the present disputed area, before the reservation period. In the 1930's when the federal government introduced tribal councils, white administrative structures were imposed on the tribes. The film contends that the tribal council pattern was introduced so that oil and mineral leases could be more easily negotiated. According to the film's analysis, the Navajo-Hopi land dispute has been promoted by whites to drive the Navajos from the huge coal deposits of Big Mountain.

Friction between the Navajo and Hopi tribes over the lands resulted in lawsuits brought by both tribal governments and the federal partitioning of the land in 1977. By this ruling an estimated ten thousand Navajos would be relocated, taking cash compensations and settling into tract housing provided for them off the reservation. Many traditional Navajos have sworn they will not leave. The film shows that the relocation process itself is a bungled, costly disaster. Among the many problems is the lack of preparation of relocatees for life off the reservation. Moved to cities far from their family networks and familiar way of life, many will be dealing with the cash economy on a day-to-day basis for the first time.

The film makes its case strongly, and undoubtedly viewers will feel angered at the harshness of the situation. An ancient, self-sufficient community of Navajos is being destroyed, and land both Hopis and Navajos see as sacred is on the brink of ecological destruction. The story told by BROKEN RAINBOW is bitter and wrenching, and the film ends with an appeal that Public Law 93-531 be overturned. The removal process is still under fire and the official date for finalizing it has been delayed.

BRUJOS AND HEALERS/BRUJOS Y CURANDEROS
For description see *Mexico Indigena Series.*

BUILDING AN ALGONKIAN BIRCHBARK CANOE
For description see *Trust for Native American Cultures and Crafts Video.*

THE BUSH TOBOGGAN
For description see *Ojibway and Cree Cultural Centre Video.*

BY THE WORK OF OUR HANDS
For description see *Choctaw Video.*

CAMINO TRISTE: THE HARD ROAD OF THE GUATEMALAN REFUGEES
1983, 30 min. Producer/directors: Nancy Peckenham and Martin Lucas. Camera: Ilan Ziv. ¾" vt, ½" vt (VHS, Beta). Color. In English or Spanish, with indigenous languages translated by subtitles. Dist.: Icarus.

Filmed in a refugee camp, this videotape focuses attention on the Maya Indians of Guatemala whose lives have been tragically disrupted by recent political and military events. An accumulation of internal tensions and struggles preceded the election of Rios Montt. When his government came into power in 1982 civil unrest intensified. Anti-government insurgents became increasingly active in the western highlands. The government's counterinsurgency program began to brutally attack the Mayan population of the area. According to international human rights groups, since these events began more than one million Guatemalans, most of them Indians, have been uprooted or killed. They have hidden in the jungles, some joining the anti-government struggle, while others have fled as refugees, mainly settling in camps in southern Mexico, such as the one in which this documentary has been filmed.

As CAMINO TRISTE shows, even Mexico offers inadequate refuge, since the camps are not funded by the Mexican government nor are foreign agencies permitted to support them. Most help up to this time has come from individuals or church organizations. Guatemalan militia and troops even move across the border to attack the refugees. In interviews, refugees speak of unprovoked attacks, brutal murders, and the slaughter of whole villages. Some of the refugees have found work with Mexican peasant farmers, recent homesteaders themselves. (Mexico has relocated landless farmers from other regions to the Lacandon forest where most of the camps are.)

The refugees are shown waiting in limbo, unable to find adequate subsistence at the camps. The memories of the brutality they have experienced in Guatemala are sustained by their isolation and by the fact that they will not be able to return safely to their homes. Although the cessation of violence has been promised for Indians of the highlands, there is continuing evidence of military hostilities against those who have remained (see description of GUATEMALA: A JOURNEY TO THE END OF MEMORIES in this volume).

CELEBRATION
and THE PIPE IS THE ALTAR
1979–80, 26 min. Producer/director: Chris Spotted Eagle. Camera: Tom Adair. Sound: Brad

Cochrane. Editors: Dan Luke and Alan Moorman. Produced by Twin Cities Public Television for the series Wyld Ryce. *Executive producer: Donald Knox. ¾" vt, ½" vt (VHS, Beta). Color. Dist.: Intermedia.*

Two companion pieces from a magazine-format television program present aspects of contemporary Native American culture for Indians living in the Minneapolis-St. Paul area. CELEBRATION (1979), filmed at the Honor the Earth Pow Wow held annually on the Lac Courte Oreilles Reservation in Wisconsin, depicts the strengths of Native American life that the powwow makes public and celebrates. Powwow dancing, feasting, give-aways, traditional Indian team sports, and even a boxing match are shown as the production explains their significance and shows communal aspects of life which are still valued today by Native Americans. In THE PIPE IS THE ALTAR (1980) spiritual leader Amos Owen, a Sioux Indian living on the Prairie Island Indian Reservation near Red Wing, Minnesota, shares his daily prayer ritual using the ceremonial pipe.

As local television public affairs programs, these works have an informal camera style and an educational explanatory narration. The producer of these pieces is a well-known Native American independent filmmaker who has specialized in reflecting views of urban and contemporary Indians to a wider public. His productions, which include THE GREAT SPIRIT WITHIN THE HOLE, HEART OF THE EARTH SURVIVAL SCHOOL, and OUR SACRED LAND (see descriptions in this volume).

CHOCTAW VIDEO

The Mississippi Band of Choctaw Indians is located in central Mississippi near the town of Philadelphia, on the only Choctaw reservation in the Southeast. The once extensive tribe was largely removed to Oklahoma in the nineteenth century. This band has experienced great poverty and in the past decade a remarkable recovery. Employment, better housing, and more control of the education of Choctaw children have resulted from a combination of strong leadership and tribal initiative, and federal programs to assist the tribe in housing and the development of income sources.

Two video production groups have been developed, one to better document Choctaw heritage, and the other a tribal enterprise which has made productions for the Choctaw and other tribal communities.

Choctaw Heritage Video

Producer: William Brescia. Assistant producer: Maria Isaac. Camera: Robert Burns, Torye Hurst, Johnny Sartin and Bryan Mask. Produced by the Choctaw Ethnic Heritage Program in cooperation with the University of Southern Mississippi. ¾" vt, ½" vt (VHS, Beta). Color. Dist.: Choctaw Heritage.

This project has produced curriculum materials and videotapes for use in classes in Mississippi history and for the general public. The tapes present Choctaw history and contemporary culture, including Choctaw Fair, Choctaw crafts, and the history of its tribal government.

BY THE WORK OF OUR HANDS *(1983, 30 min.)*

Focused on crafts, this production documents tribal members expert in making split-oak baskets, cane baskets, and drums. The narration provides background information as the artists demonstrate their methods and the use of natural materials in producing their work.

MORE THAN JUST A WEEK OF FUN *(1984, 12 min.)*

Choctaw Fair, held on the reservation every summer, provides both the tribe and non-Choctaw an opportunity for fun and a heightened awareness of the Choctaw way of life. Events shown include amusements; demonstrations of traditional Choctaw dance, crafts, and hunting with blowguns; powwow dancing; and the world championship Choctaw stickball tournament.

CHOCTAW TRIBAL GOVERNMENT *(1985, 17 min.)*

An explanation of the structure and functions of Mississippi Choctaw tribal government — its legislative, judicial, and administrative powers — and a view of life on the Choctaw reservation today are clearly presented in this production.

Choctaw Video Productions

Executive producer: Bob Ferguson. ¾" vt, ½" vt (VHS, Beta). Color. Dist.: Choctaw Video.

This tribal enterprise has produced works on several contemporary eastern tribes and their leadership, including the Mississippi Band of Choctaw Indians, the Tunica Biloxi, and the Seneca Nation of Indians. Among its productions is:

CHOCTAW STORY *(1985, 28 min.)*

The purpose of this tape is to highlight the achievement of the tribal administration of Chief Phillip Martin. Since 1979 numerous improvements have been made including new housing starts, the opening of the Choctaw Health Center, and the establishment on the reservation of a high school. The tribe has created 1000 jobs, including enterprise to manufacture greeting cards and electronic parts, with the goal of reducing Choctaw dependency on federal programs.

CHOQELA: ONLY INTERPRETATION

For description see *Mountain Music of Peru.*

CIRCLE OF THE SUN

For description see *Standing Alone.*

COME FORTH LAUGHING: VOICES OF THE SUQUAMISH PEOPLE

1983, 15 min. Produced by the Suquamish Tribal Cultural Center. Slide tape transferred to ¾" vt, ½" vt. Black-and-white and color. Dist.: Suquamish.

Many of the strongest recent productions on Native Americans provide views of elders who have fashioned from bitter past experiences a forward-looking attitude for themselves and their communities. COME FORTH LAUGHING is an excellent example of a production centered around cultural transition. Comprised of still photographs, it is narrated by members of the Suquamish Indian Tribe living in the Puget Sound region of Washington State. Through well-selected personal anecdotes and memories, they reflect on how their generation grew up, were educated in boarding schools, and were forced to discard their traditional ways and language.

Originally a slide-tape program produced by the Suquamish Museum, the piece is available for distribution on videotape. The audio component is drawn entirely from oral history interviews conducted with tribal elders by museum staff, and the images are drawn from works collected during the tribe's Photographic Archives Project. The black-and-white stills — school portraits and views of Suquamish communities and activities — date from the early decades of the century. The tape ends with a small selection replayed from each one's narration, as he or she is shown and identified through a recent color photograph. Through these personal recollections, both painful and joyful ones, COME FORTH LAUGHING makes the tribe's history and culture come alive.

CONTRARY WARRIORS: A STORY OF THE CROW TRIBE

1985, 58 min. Producers: Connie Poten and Pamela Roberts. Co-Producer: Beth Ferris. Writers: Connie Poten and Beth Ferris. Camera: Stephen Lighthill. Editor: Jennifer Chinlund. Sound: Ann Evans. Narrator: Peter Coyote. Music: Todd Boekelheide. 16mm, ½" vt (sales and rentals), ¾" vt (sales only). Color. Dist.: Direct Cinema.

This award-winning documentary on the Crow people of southeastern Montana, as told by members of the tribe, documents the life of 97-year-old Robert Yellowtail as a focus for the telling of Crow history. Its title refers to the Crow tradition of the "contrary warrior" who rode into battle backwards; if he survived, his bravery was greatly honored. Part of the tribe's survival has been due to the strong and flexible leadership of Yellowtail, who epitomizes the brave-hearted contrary warrior.

Among the first generation of Crow children born on the reservation, he taught himself law at a time when most Crow spoke no English. The Crow were already suffering under the effects of the 1887 Allotment Act which split up tribal lands, when in 1910 a bill was introduced by Montana's Senator Walsh to sell half the Crows' land to homesteaders. Yellowtail was chosen by his people to speak before Congress against the bill. After seven years of struggle his arguments prevailed, and he thus embarked on a long career as an advocate of Crow rights and tribal autonomy.

Younger tribe members offer a view of contemporary life on the reservation where the economy makes life a struggle. Women of three generations speak of the importance of the extended family and the role of women. The community provides the basis for Crow identity, a tie which difficult circumstances often cause to be breached, for people of all ages. The film records the solemnity and pride of a naming ceremony for Yellowtail's great-grandson as he prepares to join his parents who have found work off the reservation. Hank Real Bird recounts his experience with city life and how its isolation led him back to family and friends. In their sense of belonging to the tribe and to the land, the present generation seems to share the intensity of Yellowtail's lifelong commitment to the Crow people.

CONVERSATIONS IN MARANHÃO

1977/1983, 120 min. Producer/director/camera: Andrea Tonacci. Sound: Walter Luis Rogerio. Editor: Bruno de Andre. Anthropological consultants: Gilberto Azanha and Maria Luisa Ladeira. 16mm. Color. In Portuguese and Ge, with English subtitles. For distribution information contact: Tonacci.

In 1977 the Canela-Apanyekra Indians in the state of Maranhão disagreed with

20

the official demarcation of their land by the Fundação Nacional do Indio (FUNAI). As a protest they decided to interrupt the work of the surveyors and to participate in making this film, which the Canela intended as an official document in the presentation of their case to the government.

The film presents the group's history through accounts of a massacre they suffered at the hands of local landowners and the dispersion and regrouping of the survivors. Tribe members delineate the traditional boundaries of their territory and express their concern that FUNAI is ignoring these in its survey. Images of daily and ritual life, such as log-carrying duels, briefly show many aspects of Canela culture. At one point Tonacci also records the history of these lands from the settlers' viewpoint, interviewing a family in its sparse homestead.

For some viewers the lengthy oratory, which is an important part of tribal decision-making, may make the film difficult to follow. However, by documenting the contemporary situation of one group in an area whose native population has been little interviewed or filmed, this production adds significantly to a better understanding of native Brazil. Produced as a vehicle for tribal viewpoints and filmed with hand-held camera, it conveys the immediacy of the issues these Indians face. Tonacci, an award-winning Brazilian filmmaker, has also produced a documentary for Brazilian television concerned with the first contact made by FUNAI with Arara Indians in the state of Pará.

CORN IS LIFE

1982, 19 min. Producers. Therese Burson and Donald Coughlin. Director/writer: Donald Coughlin. Camera: Randy Love. Sound: Nelson Stoll. Editor: Fred Steim. Translator: Michael Lomatuway'ma. Narrator: Ramson Lomatuway'ma. Produced for the Museum of Northern Arizona. Project director: Robert Breunig. 16mm, ¾" vt, ½" vt. Color. In English or Hopi. Dist.: UCEMC.

This well-filmed documentary shows the role of corn in Hopi life as an essential food, a holy substance used in nearly all aspects of religious life, and a major cultural symbol. Ancient ways of preparing corn seed, then planting, cultivating, and harvesting the crop are shown. Not only is corn a source of subsistence, its very origin and its continued significance to the Hopi is seen as sacred. The place of the Kachina spirits in bringing needed water for its growth is illustrated by Hopi paintings of the Kachina dancers.

The film shows how older generations pass on their knowledge of ways to process and use corn. It opens with the naming ceremony of a baby, using cornmeal ceremonially, and continues with a scene in which the mother and the grandmother prepare corn, watched by the baby. It also stresses the value Hopi place on cooperative work in scenes which show women grinding corn together and preparing several special corn dishes. A grandmother makes paper-thin *piki* bread on the hot polished stone her family has used for generations. Men work to harvest corn and cermonially prepare it for preservation and eating. Such scenes present a distinct view of the significance, and difference, of men's and women's traditional roles.

At its conclusion, the film shows a family, from a young child to a great-grandfather, harvesting a field of corn together. Thus corn and its cycle of growth are seen to be inextricably intertwined with all aspects of Hopi life, symbolizing the continuation of the Hopi and their culture.

THE CRAFT OF WEAVING

For description see *Mexico Indigena Series.*

CREEK NATION VIDEO

Producer/director of all programs: Gary Robinson. Produced by the Muscogee Creek Nation Communication Center. ¾" vt, ½" vt. Color. A copy of any program is available at no charge, if a cassette is supplied, from: MCNCC.

Once part of a powerful confederacy of Indians in Georgia and Alabama, today the Creek Nation extends across seven Oklahoma counties and its tribal government is actively engaged in community development. For the past decade the Muscogee Creek Nation Communication Center, located in Okmulgee, Oklahoma, has been producing videotapes to present accurate and contemporary views of the Creek Nation. Seventeen programs on culture, history, and current affairs have been produced and shown in the state's schools and universities and on public television. For a complete list of titles and information about production services offered contact MCNCC.

Among the productions available are:

THE GREEN CORN FESTIVAL

For description see individual title.

ESTE MVSKOKE/THE MUSCOGEE PEOPLE

1985, 24 min. Associate producers: Marty Fulk and Gene Hamilton. Script: Gary Robinson. Narrator: Tim Bigpond. A co-production of MCNCC and the Oklahoma Indian Education Department. Additional dist.: ODE.

Beginning with the "origin of clans," this program provides an overview of the history, culture, and modern achievements of the Creek Nation. Parts of the Green Corn Festival and a stickball game are shown, and the role of Creek churches is also stressed.

FOLKLORE OF THE MUSCOGEE PEOPLE

1983, 28 min. Writer: Gary Robinson. Camera: Trish Popkess. Technical director: Jim Reid. Narrator: Ruth Arrington. A co-production of MCNCC and KOED-TV, Tulsa. Executive producer: Rex Daugherty. Additional dist.: NAPBC.

This program focuses on six traditional Creek stories, illustrated by Indian artists, and explains the importance of the tales.

STICKBALL: THE LITTLE BROTHER OF WAR

1985, 12 min. Camera: Gary Robinson and Scott Swearingen.

A lively game of stickball is played by the men and boys of several Creek tribal towns. An explanation of this ancient Creek ceremonial sport is provided as the game takes place.

THE STRENGTH OF LIFE

For description see individual title.

1,000 YEARS OF MUSCOGEE ART

1982, 28 min. Writer: Bruce Shackleford. Narrator: Mike Bigler. Additional dist.: NAPBC.

This program surveys the development of Creek art forms, including clothing, pottery, jewelry, basketry, sculpture, painting, and engraving.

TURTLE SHELLS

1986, 26 min. Camera/editor: Gary Robinson. Narrator: Ruth Arrington.

Although turtle shell rattles are still an important part of the traditional dance dress of Creek women, today few are skilled in making them. This videotape documents Christine Henneha making a set of rattles, from catching the turtles and processing the shells to preparing them to be worn as leggings.

DAVID CHARLES

For description see *Ojibway and Cree Cultural Centre Video.*

DOCTORA

1983, 52 min. Producer/directors: Linda Post and Eugene Rosow. Camera: Antonio Eguino. Sound: Alberto Villanpando. Editor: Eugene Rosow. Produced for Channel 4, Great Britain. 16mm, ¾" vt. Color. Dist.: Post-Rosow.

A portrait of Ruth Tichauer, M.D., whose 40-year practice in Bolivia has included a deep commitment to comprehensive health care for native peoples there. Born in Germany, Dr. Tichauer came to Bolivia with her family in 1940–41. She established a practice in a middle class neighborhood in La Paz. Seeing that the poor lacked medical help, in 1946 she also opened a clinic in the large Indian quarter of La Paz. She does not romanticize her role, stating clearly that "the patients I feel good with happen to be Aymara."

The impact of the "Doctora" is described by various leaders of the community and by her staff who are all from the neighborhood. The team works in the city and, on invitation, goes to rural farming and mining communities. DOCTORA shows how a non-Indian can offer much-needed professional services to a native population and can assist members of the community served to realize their own professional skills. Although some aspects of her life have undoubtedly been difficult, Dr. Tichauer speaks with contentment and humility, "We are normal people with professional training—it is our luck to have found something so satisfying to ourselves and others, too."

THE DRUM

For description see *Ojibway and Cree Cultural Centre Video.*

THE DRUM IS THE HEART

1982, 29 min. Producer/photographer: Randy Croce. A project of MIGIZI Communications, Minneapolis. Slide tape transferred to ¾" vt, ½" vt. Color. Dist.: Intermedia.

The Blackfoot nation consists of four groups, the Blackfeet of Montana and, on reserves in Canada, the Northern Blackfoot, Blood, and Piegan. Focused on the theme that the enduring values of the Blackfoot Nation are expressed in their modern-day celebrations, this production by professional photographer Randy Croce is the result of seven years of recording annual summer powwows in Alberta and in Montana. The narration is chosen from interviews with numerous Blackfoot people of all ages and was selected after screening of the slide program for Blackfoot audiences.

The many beautiful photographs show ceremonial costumes, tipi interiors, painting of tipi covers, and interactions between people of all ages. Glen Eaglespeaker, tipi painter and traditional dancer of the Blood tribe, speaks of the antiquity of the tipi, although today canvas, not hide, is used in its making. Nell Kipp, Blackfeet tribal historian, speaks of the pride engendered by powwows. Maynard Kicking Woman decribes what the production strongly demonstrates about the continuity and contemporary relevance of Indian traditions, "The Indian people are beginning to dig deeper . . . and bringing out all that old stuff. But when they bring it out, they modernize it."

THE EARTH IS OUR HOME
1979, 29 min. Producer/writer: Elizabeth Patapoff. Camera: Uli Kretzschmar. Produced by Oregon Public Broadcasting. 16mm, ¾'' vt, ½'' vt (VHS, Beia). Dist.: OPB (sales only)/MP (sales and rentals).

This film was produced in cooperation with members of the Burns Paiute tribe in Oregon to preserve a record of their traditional way of life and skills. The ancestors of the Northern Paiute were one of a number of tribes who made up what is referred to as the Great Basin culture, found in Nevada, Utah, and parts of seven other western states. In this arid area, unsuitable for agriculture, the people lived by hunting, gathering, and fishing. To obtain their subsistence they utilized during the changing seasons of the year different environments, including desert, rugged foothills, and salt marshes.

THE EARTH IS OUR HOME provides an excellent in-depth view of a Native American adaptation to a regional ecology describing the seasonal use of plants and animals, as well as techniques of food preparation and manufacture of articles used for subsistence. Northern Paiute women share memories of old ways and demonstrate making twined and coiled basketry, cordage, a duck decoy, a rabbitskin robe, and a cattail shelter. They are shown collecting foods such as camus and bitterroot, and processing chokecherries and aphids, from which a sweet liquid can be obtained.

ELLA MAE BLACKBEAR: CHEROKEE BASKETMAKER
1982, 25 min. Producer/director/editors: Scott Swearingen and Sheila Swearingen. Narrator: Fran Ringold. ¾'' vt, ½'' vt (VHS, Beta). Color. Dist.: Full Circle (sales only).

Ella Mae Blackbear practices the ancient art of Cherokee basketmaking as it has survived in Oklahoma after the Cherokees' removal to the Indian Territory in the late 1830's. The artist, whose work is sought by museums and collectors, returned late in life to the basketry skills she learned as a small child from her mother. Filmed on location in rural northeastern Oklahoma, the videotape has the quality of an informal visit to the artist's home. It opens with the collection of the buck brush plant and the blood root flower, some of the natural materials used in making the baskets. The artist's warmth and accessibility make a strong impression as she talks of her life and work while the videomakers document her weaving.

After gathering the materials she may boil the buck brush for as long as twenty hours. This done, she strips the runners, dyes them with natural dyes, and finally weaves them into the basket. The production concludes with what might be considered the final step in the production of native baskets today, their sale to tourists and afficionados of Indian art. Although baskets no longer serve the wide variety of functional uses in Cherokee life they once did, their production is still a highly valued aspect of Cherokee tradition, and one which Ella Mae Blackbear hopes her daughter and other young people will want to continue.

EMERGENCE

1981, 14 min. Producer/writer/animator: Barbara Wilk. 16 mm, ¾" vt, ½" vt. Color animation. Dist.: Barr/Centre.

EMERGENCE tells the story of the events leading to the entrance of the Dineh, the Navajo people, onto the surface of this earth through a number of underworlds. Though there are many versions of these origin myths, sacred to the Navajo, the film presents themes common to them all. It tells how the supernaturals — in particular, the First Pair, Coyote, Talking God, and Black God — assisted humans and other living beings to change and develop. The animation is dense with images from the tale, its drawings based on ceremonial sand painting and ancient pictographs. Sacred colors, cardinal directions, the sacred mountains representing the earth's body which are inhabited by holy beings, and the four sacred plants are all evoked.

The traditional chants heard in the film are versions of the origin myths sung as part of certain Navajo healing rituals. Because they are used in a ceremonial context, and during the winter only, the filmmaker has requested that this film be screened only during the winter months. An informative study guide is available upon request. Other animations by Wilk include LETTER FROM AN APACHE (see description this volume) and QUEEN VICTORIA AND THE INDIANS (Dist.: Barr/Centre).

THE ENCHANTED ARTS: PABLITA VELARDE

1977, 28 min. Producer/director: Irene-Aimee Depke. Camera: Pat Holian and Jim Ficklin. Produced for KRWT-TV, Las Cruces, NM. Executive producer/director: Jim Ficklin. ¾" vt. Color. Dist.: Depke.

One of the first Indian women to pursue painting professionally, artist Pablita Velarde holds an enduring place in the history of Native American art. Only a few years after graduation from the United States Indian School in Santa Fe, where she was a student of Dorothy Dunn, Velarde was chosen by the Work Projects Administration to produce a series of paintings between 1939 and 1948 at Bandelier National Monument in New Mexico. During her long career, she has continued to paint, as well as to sculpt clay figures. Recently, she has begun "earth painting," using natural earth pigments which she grinds on a traditional grinding stone, as shown in this production.

THE ENCHANTED ARTS presents an engaging portrait of the artist, in part because of Velarde's willingness to discuss significant aspects of her personal history in an open manner. She emerges from the interviews as an independent women who pursued her art despite criticisms that painting was not considered appropriate for a woman. Although sometimes at odds with the traditions of her Santa Clara Pueblo upbringing, she nevertheless has made a major contribution as an interpreter of life in her own and other Pueblos. The delight

Velarde takes in the Pueblo imagination is seen in the production's closing scenes, as she tells a Coyote tale to a group of young Indian children.

THE END OF THE RACE

1981, 27 min. Producer/director: Hector Galan. Camera: Jiri Tirl. Editor: Larry Ross. Narrator: Mike McKinnon. Produced by the Southwest Center for Educational Television. Executive producer: Frederick P. Close. ¾" vt. Color. Dist.: SCET.

For many Indian peoples, running holds a significant place in culture and religion. Perhaps nowhere is this more important than among Pueblo Indians. THE END OF THE RACE profiles four Pueblo championship cross-country runners. It also explores Pueblo values, stressing the significance of the family and spiritual beliefs, and discusses the difficulties posed by the encroachment of the majority culture.

Ine lives and attitudes of the runners—Steven Gachupin, Meldon Sanchez, Andy Martinez, and Al Waqui—provide the viewer with insight into Pueblo values. Today running is rooted in the Pueblo ceremonial foot race, in which the goal of winning is secondary to insuring that all participants finish. Traditional Pueblo culture does not stress the competitive ethos valued by white society. A former coach at the Laguna-Acoma High School sees the indifference of many Pueblo young people to educational achievement to be a result of the educational system's insistence on competitive behavior.

Young people are also discouraged because there are rarely good employment opportunities within Pueblo communities. Attempts to introduce industry have often failed. At Laguna Pueblo, for example, a mining enterprise offered jobs only temporarily and produced dangerous waste and erosion. As shown by a lively family meal with classic Pueblo dishes, close family ties are greatly valued. Although necessary for economic survival, employment elsewhere imposes great hardship on the people.

Interwoven with interviews and scenes of life is commentary about the central importance of sacred values for Pueblo Indians. The production concludes with observations about the religious roots of Pueblo running and the privacy which surrounds its more profound meaning. Through its examination of running, this production explores contemporary Pueblo life, discussing issues of continued economic and cultural survival and presenting a view of the strength of traditional values.

ESTE MVSKOKE

For description see *Creek Nation Video.*

EVERY DAY CHOICES: ALCOHOL AND AN ALASKA TOWN

1985, 93 min. Producer/director/editor: Sarah Elder. Camera: Cristine Burrill. Second camera: Leonard Kamerling. Researcher/production manager: Katrina Kassler. Produced for the Alaska Native Heritage Film Project. Executive producers: Sarah Elder and Leonard Kamerling. 16mm, ¾" vt, ½" vt. Color. In English and Yup'ik with English voice-over. Dist.: Northern Heritage.

On the Kuskokwim River in southwestern Alaska, Bethel serves as the urban center for 51 Yup'ik Eskimo villages located in an area larger than New England. In this documentary, award-winning filmmaker Sarah Elder takes on one of the most difficult problems facing Native Americans today—alcoholism. In the 1970's Elder and filmmaker Leonard Kamerling founded the Alaska Native Heritage Film Project which pioneered the co-production of films with native villagers. Like the earlier films in the project, EVERY DAY CHOICES features excellent interviews. Without narration it presents the realities of Inuit life in terms the people themselves suggest.

EVERY DAY CHOICES shows how insidious, destructive, and pervasive the problem of alcohol is in native communities in the north. Its audience, both Native American and non-native, is led to consider what the human costs of modern changes imposed upon native peoples have been. The film addresses stereotyped ideas of Native American alcoholism by showing how much these victims of alcohol want to have more control over their lives. A number of different situations in the town are shown, including various facilities for the care and treatment of alcoholics. The film follows the struggle of one man to be cured of his disease.

The Alaska Native Heritage Film Project (for additional information see description in Volume I, p. 13) is soon to end because of budget cuts. Its final productions portray elders from three villages and traditional Yup'ik Eskimo dance and beliefs. For further information contact the distributor.

EYES OF THE SPIRIT

1984, 28 min. Producer/writer: Corey Flintoff. Director/camera: Alexie Isaac. Narrator: Ina Carpenter. Produced by KYUK-TV, Bethel, AK. All video formats. Color. Dist.: KYUK. For additional information see KYUK VIDEO.

For the Yup'ik Eskimo of southwest Alaska, the dance tradition included the use of carved wooden masks of great beauty and complexity. Many of these masterpieces, once used in shamanic ritual, are now found in museum collections. Under the influence of Christian missionaries, the people put aside much of their customary spiritual beliefs and in some areas dancing ceased altogether. Although masks continued to be made for tourists and collectors, the forms changed since they were no longer being worn for dancing.

In 1982 a group of dancers and carvers active in preserving and teaching Yup'ik traditions, the Bethel Native Dancers, received a grant from the Alaska State Council on the Arts to revive the use of masks in their dancing. Three master carvers were commissioned to make masks, and young apprentices came to learn from them. EYES OF THE SPIRIT documents their work.

The program imparts the spirit in which the carvers are working, giving much information about the techniques and materials used to produce the masks, as well as the roles of masks and dance in the past. The carvers teach by example, highlighting the sense that this project is an expression of values at the culture's core. Directed by a Yup'ik television producer, the program reflects the continuing efforts of people in this region to maintain their cultural traditions and to gain greater control over their communities' economic and political future.

FACES OF CULTURE SERIES

1983, 29 min. each program. Series producer: Ira Abrams. Creative consultant: Arthur Barron. Series narrator: David Carradine. Produced by the Coast Community Colleges (KOCE-TV, Huntington Beach, CA) in cooperation with Holt, Rinehart and Winston, and in association with five institutions and consortia. Executive producer: Sandra Austin Harden. ¾" vt. Color. Dist.: Coast.

With the increased use of televised college courses and audiovisual materials for classroom instruction, this series provides a complete film course in cultural anthropology, demonstrating the important concepts of anthropology in an engaging manner. FACES OF CULTURE consists of 26 broadcast-quality programs, which are organized thematically following the table of contents of the text they are intended to accompany, William Haviland's *Cultural Anthropology.*

The film footage used in the programs is taken from archival and recent ethnographic films and projects, expertly edited to suit the format of the program. It employs good selections from films using current ideas of documentation. The majority of programs with Native American material are case studies of particular topics, focused on one family or tribal location. As noted, the original films from which these programs were drawn are described in NATIVE AMERICANS ON FILM AND VIDEO.

ALEJANDRO MAMANI:
A CASE STUDY IN CULTURE AND PERSONALITY

Writer: Hubert Smith

By examining a Bolivian Aymara man suffering with mental illness, this program shows that the shape of his illness reflects conditions of Aymara life and its system of beliefs. (See FACES OF CHANGE SERIES in Volume I, p. 44–45.)

THE AYMARA: A CASE STUDY IN SOCIAL STRATIFICATION

Writer: Hubert Smith

This program examines class stratification through the documentation of a community of Aymara Indians in the Bolivian Andes and their relationship with the middle class inhabitants of the rural towns of their area. Both groups are interdependent and yet, for the Aymara, barriers to mobility and differences in education, health care, and economies have led to a permanent class difference. (See FACES OF CHANGE SERIES in Volume I, p. 44–45.)

THE HIGHLAND MAYA:
A CASE STUDY IN ECONOMIC ANTHROPOLOGY

Writer: Anne Robinson Taylor

The Maya Indians of the highlands of Mexico and Guatemala maintain a unique economic system that combines religious practices, the bearing of community responsibilities, and social prestige. Noted anthropologist Frank Cancian discusses the function of the *cargo* system. While generally beneficial, it also reinforces inequalities between the Maya and their neighbors. Through footage selected from a number of films, this production shows the celebration of the fiestas in which cargo duties are carried out and probes the contemporary Maya way of life. (See APPEALS TO SANTIAGO in Volume I, p. 17, and TODOS SANTOS CUCHUMATAN in this volume.)

THE YUCATEC MAYA:
A CASE STUDY IN MARRIAGE AND THE FAMILY

Writer: Hubert Smith

This program looks at the Colli Colli family, contemporary Maya living in the

Yucatan, and the roles of each family member in providing for the group's subsistence. Anthropologist Hubert Smith reflects on his presence as participant observer. The program discusses the pressures facing this family as modern changes make an impact on their lives and their expectations for the future. (See MAYA OF CONTEMPORARY YUCATAN SERIES (THE LIVING MAYA), Volume I, p. 76–77.)

Other programs include selected footage of Native Americans:

CULTURE CHANGE (Pueblo)

KINSHIP AND DESCENT (Hopi and Inuit)

NEW ORLEANS' BLACK INDIANS (examines a Mardi Gras dance club whose members attribute their ancestry in part to Indians)

RELIGION AND MAGIC (Navajo)

FOLKLORE OF THE MUSCOGEE CREEK
For description see Creek Nation Video.

THE FOUR CORNERS: A NATIONAL SACRIFICE AREA?
1983, 59 min. Producer/directors: Christopher McLeod, Glenn Switkes, and Randy Hayes. 16mm, ¾" vt, ½" vt. Color. Dist.: Bullfrog.

The Four Corners area of Utah, Colorado, New Mexico, and Arizona is rich in history for Native Americans whose traditional homelands are there and for the descendants of its American settlers. This ninety thousand square miles of the Colorado Plateau is also rich in coal and oil shale and shelters half of America's uranium reserves. In addition, this region is the site of the Golden Circle of national parks and rugged canyon lands.

THE FOUR CORNERS raises questions about the "hidden costs" of energy development in the Southwest, taking its title from a National Academy of Sciences report which concludes that reaching energy self-sufficiency in the United States could result in decisions to extract resources from some areas which would ultimately become uninhabitable, i.e., "nationally sacrificed." The film features interesting interviews with a broad spectrum of the region's inhabitants and leaders — Navajo uranium miners, tribal officers, governors, ranchers, energy company spokesmen, and federal government officials. Their comments bring home the powerful conflicts which surround the issues of energy, environment, and human well-being in the Southwest.

The serious problems of each extractive industry are touched upon. Uranium, and its wastes, have left the Navajo reservation full of radioactive tailings, and with high incidences of lung cancer and birth defects among Navajo and Hopi Indians. In addition, the national parks are threatened by the stripmining of coal and the potential construction of large power plants. Water is being contaminated throughout the Colorado River Basin; these sources supply Los Angeles, Phoenix, and much of the Southwest.

The film is a thoughtful investigation, supplying no easy answers. Even at a time of reduced discussion of energy self-sufficiency in the United States, pressures to develop federal lands and increase the exploitation of Indian lands in the American West still continue. By asking if the short-term gains of the energy projects for this area are worth the hidden costs, it poses a serious challenge to government policies. Perhaps for this reason, at its release, the head of the National Endowment for the Humanities publicly criticized the Arizona Humanities Council for financially supporting the film. Meanwhile, THE FOUR CORNERS, produced by three students in journalism, won the 1984 Student Academy Award for Documentary.

FROM HAND TO HAND: BETHEL NATIVE ARTIST PROFILES

1985, entire series: 45 min. (each segment: approximately 10 min.). Producer/camera/editor: Gretchen McManus. Associate producer/sound: Elizabeth Mayock. Narrator: Martha Larson. Produced by KYUK-TV and the Yugtarvik Regional Museum, Bethel, AK. Executive producer: John A. McDonald. ¾" vt, ½" vt. Color. In Yup'ik or English. Dist.: KYUK. For additional information see KYUK VIDEO.

This series, available separately or on one videocassette, consists of short profiles of Yup'ik Eskimo artists and their work. It has been produced for a regional museum located at Bethel in southwestern Alaska. Featuring practitioners who discuss the place of their art in traditional Yup'ik culture, these productions make a lively statement about contemporary Yup'ik life.

STORYKNIFING documents a unique storytelling tradition in which a blade is used to cut images in the mud or snow to accompany the telling. The tradition is handed down to little girls from older sisters, mothers, and grandmothers. Martha Larson tells about this art through her memories and reflections, and Esther Green tells a story to a group of little girls. One participant jokes that this is how all the table knives in a Yup'ik household get misplaced.

In LUCY BEAVER, SKIN SEWER a remarkable elder shows her skill and describes many aspects of her life. She observes that the designs with which she decorates skin garments are in the style of designs drawn in storyknifing.

In NICK CHARLES, CARVER the artist, who is from Nelson Island, discusses his life as he carves a mask. In UNCLE JOHN, CARVER a master carver from Nunivak Island makes a dance mask and talks about his craft. His masks, in the traditional style of the Yup'ik, are used today by the Bethel Native Dancers in their performances. Another documentary featuring Uncle John is EYES OF THE SPIRIT (see description in this volume).

THE GIFT OF THE SACRED DOG

1983, 30 min. Producer: Cecily Truett. Director: Larry Lancit. Series host: LeVar Burton. Narrator: Michael Ansara. Produced by Lancit Media Productions. The series Reading Rainbow is a co-production of Great Plains National Television Library and WNED-TV, Buffalo. Executive producers: Twila Ligget and Tony Buttino. ¾" vt, ½" vt. Color. Dist.: GPN.

Funded by the Corporation for Public Broadcasting and nationally broadcast, the Reading Rainbow series acquaints young readers with well-chosen, easy-to-read books. GIFT OF THE SACRED DOG, written and illustrated by Paul Goble, provides the basis for a program focused on Native Americans. The narrator reads the book as its illustrations are shown, presenting a tale of ancient times told with minor variations by several tribes of the Great Plains, in which a boy brings to his people the first horse, known to some tribes as the "sacred dog."

The program expands on themes introduced by the book. A documentary film sequence presents Dan Old Elk and his family who live at Crow Agency, Montana, and shows them preparing for and participating in the festivities of the annual Crow Indian Fair, including tipi raising and powwow dancing.

Brief reviews of related books are given by three children, including a traditional African tale, a photographic essay on Native American life, and a Japanese tale of a boy and his horse. The program concludes with host LeVar Burton, who is enthusiastic and interesting throughout, discussing Indian family names and inviting the young viewers to consider how language and names are vital to a sense of cultural identity. Other *Reading Rainbow* programs that include books with Native American stories or characters are KEEP THE LIGHT BURNING, ABBY; HILL OF FIRE; and PAUL BUNYAN.

GIVEAWAY AT RING THUNDER

1982, 15 min. Producer/writer: Jan Wahl. Writer/narrator/editor: Christine Lesiak. Camera: Tim Harton. Produced for Nebraska Educational Television. ½" vt. Color. Dist.: NETV (sales only).

This production opens with archival photographs of Lakota Sioux life and a reflection on traditional customs in earlier times. Originally, as a sign of the end of mourning, a deceased person's family would give away all its goods to the rest of the community. Over the years the formal giving of gifts came to be held for many reasons, such as when children are born or a family wishes to show its gratitude for good fortune.

A giveaway held during the annual Ring Thunder powwow on the Rosebud Sioux Reservation in South Dakota is documented. The Menard family is celebrating the giving of Indian names to three children. Early photographs, interesting interviews, and views of the powwow encampment and celebration make this a fine documentary. It defines the giveaway as at the heart of Sioux tradition and as a way for a family, through sharing, to strengthen its ties to the community. Preparations, feasting, powwow dancing, speeches, the naming ceremonial, and the giveaway are all shown. Al Menard, who has returned for his family's celebration and the powwow, and his uncle Francis, who is the give-away sponsor, provide the explanation for the event and its value for the Sioux today.

THE GREAT SPIRIT WITHIN THE HOLE

1983, 60 min. Producer/director: Chris Spotted Eagle. Camera: Michael Chin. Editor: Irving Saraf. Music: Buffy Sainte-Marie. Narrator: Will Sampson, Jr. Produced by KTCA-TV, St. Paul, MN. Executive producer: Richard O. Moore. 16mm, ¾" vt. Color. Dist.: Intermedia.

This documentary, by a noted Native American independent filmmaker, demonstrates how native spiritual practice has powerfully altered the lives of Indian prisoners in the correction facilities which have permitted it. The film not only advocates enlightened prison practices, it also testifies to the terrible human cost for Native Americans living in a society which does not comprehend their cultures, values, or histories.

The inmates, some with bitter criminal experiences, speak openly, often eloquently, of their pasts. None have had access to a culturally rich Native American upbringing and all have experienced racism first-hand. Their accounts underscore how the disruption of Native American family and community is related to the lack of a strong, positive identity for many Indian young people and contributes to violence directed toward others and themselves.

Spotted Eagle is a compassionate interviewer and his subjects seem at ease before the camera. Most of the men and women interviewed are involved with Indian spiritual practices for the first time but now see as central to their survival the identity and sense of belonging that has come through ritual sweats, worship with the sacred pipe, and other observances.

After viewing the film, one wishes to know more about what will happen to these people. Will their new spiritual involvement sustain them against the forces that depleted them earlier in their lives? The dilemma of cultural misunderstanding and prejudice that the film addresses is seen in the fact that the practice of Native American religious activities in prisons became possible only in 1978, through special legislation passed by Congress, the American Indian Religious Freedom Act.

Spotted Eagle has made other productions concerned with contemporary Native American life and issues, including CELEBRATION, HEART OF THE EARTH SURVIVAL SCHOOL, and OUR SACRED LAND (see descriptions in this volume).

THE GREEN CORN FESTIVAL

1982, 20 min. Producer/director: Gary Robinson. Narrator: Mike Bigler. Produced by the Muscogee Creek Nation Communications Center. ¾" vt, ½" vt. Color. Dist.: MCNCC. For additional information see CREEK NATION VIDEO.

The Green Corn Festival is a celebration practiced today by the Creek at a dozen or so ceremonial grounds in Oklahoma. The videotape opens with archival footage shot in the 1940's, underscoring the longevity of the ceremonial. Everything in the festival is done in sets of four — four powers, four winds, four shelters on the grounds, and four parts to the dances.

First the women are honored with a ribbon dance, followed by a friendship dance which can include visitors. Dancing can continue all night. In the next stages of the festival men prepare a new fire, and the herbal medicine used in the ceremony is applied to ritual scratches on the legs and arms of the participants. Even young children participate, as seen when men gently administer the scratches to a small boy.

This videotape is filmed and edited simply, with many long sequences of the ceremonial activities. A succinct narration explains many of the details shown. As most ritual practices of tribes originating in the Southeast have not been filmed, this is a particularly valuable addition to media available on contemporary Native American ritual and on the Creek Nation.

GUATEMALA: A JOURNEY TO THE END OF MEMORIES

1986, 56 min. Producer/director/camera/editor: Ilan Ziv. Associate producer: Nancy Peckenham. Sound/translator: Martin Lucas. Produced in association with WDR-German Television and IKON TV-Holland. In Spanish with subtitles in English or French. ¾" vt, ½" vt (VHS, Beta). Color. Dist.: Icarus.

This work continues an investigation, begun in an earlier production, of the situation which forced thousands of Guatemalan Indians to flee their highland homes and seek refuge in countries such as Mexico and the United States. When José, a man they have met in a Mexican refugee camp, asks for advice about returning to his country following the recent declaration of amnesty for refugees, the producers decide to go to Guatemala and to return with images and information for him.

The massive killings and militarism which characterized the regime of the former Guatemalan leader, General Rios Montt, have been publicly declaimed since the election of a civilian president. The videomakers' task was to document what actually has happened to the Maya in Guatemala and to investigate their current situation in the highlands. The picture they record is not reassuring. Human rights activists in Guatemala City testify to the disappearances, which the government continues to ignore, not only of Indian villagers, but also of middle-class Guatemalans, labor leaders, and church workers.

The tension-filled journey provides a unique look at the Guatemalan highlands today. In the course of their search the crew visits "model villages" (settlements built by the army for the population displaced from their original villages), the town of Chajul where José was a catechist for a year, and a "re-education camp" the army has designed for those it considers hard-core guerrilla supporters. The journey finally reaches José's home village, destroyed by the army in 1981 and replaced by a "model village," but apparently none of the original inhabitants can be found. The crew is followed, and assumes that the chance of endangering those who speak with them is great.

The videomakers return to Mexico. When the images are screened, many people in them are known by the refugees. The tape gives an alarming view of what "pacification" continues to mean, and reminds its viewers that the situation of Guatemalan Indian peasants warrants continued press coverage and political analysis. This production is a sequel to an earlier work on the Maya refugee camps in Mexico, CAMINO TRISTE (see description in this volume).

GUATEMALA PERSONAL TESTIMONIES
For description see *When the Mountains Tremble.*

HAA SHAGOON
1983, 29 min. Producer/director/writer: Joseph Kawaky. Camera: Harry Dawson and Phil Cook. Editor: Laura Louis. Produced in cooperation with the Chilkoot Indian Association, Haines, AK. 16mm, ¾" vt, ½" vt (VHS, Beta). Color. In English and Tlingit with English subtitles. Dist.: UCEMC.

In HAA SHAGOON the Chilkat Tlingit of southeastern Alaska use a traditional ritual, the Peace Ceremony, as a vehicle to call attention to injustices against their community. In a series of dreams elder Austin Hammond had been instructed to hold the ceremony to express the Tlingits' feelings about their ancestral lands and its current mistreatment. Hammond asked Joseph Kawaky, who had never before made a film, to document the ceremony, which was held in 1982. Kawaky spent the next three years with elders researching and producing the film.

The Chilkat Tlingit no longer hold title to most of their traditional lands near the Chilkoot River and Chilkoot Lake. In the ceremony they make four requests to the state of Alaska, having to do with these ancestral lands and rights. The people ask that their ancient cemetery, disturbed by road-building, be protected; that their sacred peace rock, blasted apart during the road's construction, be restored; that they be allowed to use the Chilkoot River for subsistence fishing; and that a fish weir hampering the salmon's access to spawning grounds be removed.

Hammond speaks out eloquently against the threat to Tlingit culture. He explains the importance to today's Tlingits of their ancestors and traditional use of the land, connections expressed in the songs, dances, and oratory of the

ceremony. Ceremonial clothing bearing clan symbols and other natural and su-
pernatural beings depicts, in Hammond's words, "the ownership and history
of our land."

The film ends with the Peace Ceremony not completed, to be finished
only with the settlement of the issues presented. Because of the Tlingits' making
their appeal public, assisted by the use of this film, the state has responded to
some of their requests. The peace rock has been put back together. Plans to widen
the road through the cemetery have been abandoned, with the Tlingit receiving
title to an additional area of their burial grounds. The state also granted the
Tlingits' culture camp a permit for subsistence fishing in the Chilkoot River.
As a result, the Peace Ceremony was finally completed in the summer of 1983.

HAROLD OF ORANGE

*1983, 32 min. Producer: Dianne Brennan. Director: Richard Weise. Writer: Gerald Vizenor.
Camera: Gregory M. Cummins. Editor: Steven E. Rivkin. Music: Buffy Sainte-Marie. Pro-
duced by Film in the Cities, Minneapolis. 16mm, ¾" vt, ½" vt (VHS, Beta). Color. Dist.:
Film in the Cities.*

Produced by an independent media center in Minneapolis, with a script by a
Chippewa author and scholar, HAROLD OF ORANGE was selected by the
Sundance Institute to receive assistance in script development. It confronts with
ironic humor the issue of the interconnection between reservation communities
and the powerful bureaucracies on which they often must rely, presenting both
a group of young Indian "tricksters" and a well-intentioned, though woefully
paternalistic, white institution.

Harold Sinseer, played by Oneida Indian comedian Charlie Hill, is the
leader of the Warriors of Orange. Using wit and humor as their weapons, he
and his group disarm a white foundation, a symbol of the dominant society's
reserve of power and capital. The Warriors present a fund-raising proposal to
the foundation for the development of a chain of reservation coffee houses. They
escort the foundation directors on a "fact-finding" trip which includes a visit
to the anthropological section of a museum, a spoof of a naming ceremony, and
a softball game between the directors and the Indians, in which Harold makes
pointed remarks about the historical competitions between Indian and whites.
HAROLD OF ORANGE ridicules the society's racism and shows that innovative, even outrageous, means may be necessary to resist its deadly effect. Through
its humorous treatment, applied to both Indians' and whites' behavior and mo-
tives, the film makes an unusual and multifaceted comment on contemporary
Native American life.

HAUDENOSAUNEE: WAY OF THE LONGHOUSE

*1982, 13 min. Producer/directors: Robert Stiles and John Akin. Writers: Richard Mazza and
Ron La France. Camera: Robert Stiles and Peter Sinclair. Narrators: Frances Boots and Oren
Lyons. 16mm (sales and rentals), ¾" vt, ½" vt (sales only). Color. Dist.: Icarus.*

The traditional culture of the six nations of the Iroquois Confederacy, the League
of the Haudenosaunee, is introduced in this documentary produced for the benefit
of the Akwesasne Freedom School on the St. Regis-Akwesasne (Mohawk) reservation. Concerned with showing the value of traditional ways, the film also documents the resiliency of Iroquois culture in the face of pressures to assimilate.

Lyrical opening shots of a wooded lake lead to the interior of a longhouse

34

in which people attired in traditional-looking clothing re-enact a scene from the past as they gather around a fire to listen to a young man's oration. The matrilineal (here called "matriarchal") organization of family, clan, and society is explained, and changes in social structure are related to the steady loss of lands to Euro-American encroachment. These references to history are complemented by scenes of many contemporary Iroquois at their activities — students, teachers, artists, athletes, farmers, and professionals.

A narrator then explains the principles and concepts which underlie traditional Haudenosaunee culture and way of life, stressing the people's spiritual relationship to the land and the natural world. The film concludes with shots of a confrontation between Mohawk traditionalists and opponents within their community. This footage, with images of factories and industrial wastes, suggests that the continuation of Iroquois culture is being threatened seriously by non-Iroquois values and society.

This (and a less successful companion film, AKWESASNE: ANOTHER POINT OF VIEW) was produced in close cooperation with traditional members of the Onondaga community in New York State and the Akwesasne community on the New York-Canada border. The information presented in HAUDENO-SAUNEE is brief, but its images and clear, simple explanation should be of interest to young viewers. The film's message is one that many Native Americans would like to communicate to their own youth and to non-natives — the strength of their contemporary culture is drawn from the people's continuing knowledge and practice of their own traditions.

HEART OF THE EARTH SURVIVAL SCHOOL
and CIRCLE OF THE WINDS

1979–80, 32 min. Producer/director: Chris Spotted Eagle. Camera: Tom Adair. Sound: Brad Cochrane. Editors: Dan Luke and Alan Moorman. Produced by Twin Cities Public Television for the series Wyld Ryce. Executive producer: Donald Knox. ¾" vt, ½" vt (VHS, Beta). Color. Dist.: Intermedia.

Two productions from a public affairs television program present aspects of contemporary Native American culture for Indians living in the Minneapolis-St. Paul area. The first program (1980) documents an alternative Native American school in Minneapolis and shows how it offers many young Indians a chance to feel comfortable and become achievers for the first time in a school setting. The Heart of the Earth Survival School places strong emphasis on basic academic skills and on learning Native American history and culture. Interviews with students and teachers and scenes of classes and activities are included. Indian leaders in the community involved with the school also speak of their hopes for the lives of these young people. CIRCLE OF THE WINDS (1979), which documents a Native American student art exhibition, is a less dynamic work.

Both programs, focused on Native American education, were intended to show a wide audience what cultural survival can mean for an urban Indian community and its individual members, both adults and young people. Produced by a Native American filmmaker noted for his films on contemporary issues, the programs are part of a television series designed to present the positive accomplishments of Native Americans today. Other productions by Spotted Eagle include CELEBRATION, THE GREAT SPIRIT WITHIN THE HOLE, and OUR SACRED LAND (see descriptions in this volume).

HIKURI NEIRRA: LA DANZA DEL PEYOTE
For description see *Mexico Indigena Series.*

HIKURI-TAME
For description see *Maria Sabina: Mujer Espiritu.*

HOME OF THE BRAVE
1985, 58 min. Producer/director: Helena Solberg Ladd. Writer: David Meyer. Camera: Michael Anderson. Narrator: Ilka Tanya Pagan. 16mm, ¾" vt, ½" vt. Color. Dist.: Cinema Guild.

HOME OF THE BRAVE examines Indian leadership today and Native Americans' increasing political awareness. By calling attention to the common history and philosophy of Indian peoples in North and South America — a concern for the land as the source of life and as crucial to their continuation as a people — it is a unique documentary of contemporary native life throughout the Western Hemisphere.

HOME OF THE BRAVE first visits the Amazon region of eastern Ecuador which is targeted for development. Six tribes live here, numbering many thousands, and the development of natural resources and settlement directly threaten Indians' continued use of their lands. Asserting the need for the protection of Indian rights, leaders speak of the effect of centuries of exposure to outside control that has taught their people resignation.

In the United States land and the survival of native traditions is also a critical issue. The film examines the situation at Big Mountain in northern Arizona where Navajo elders face removal from lands they have inhabited for many generations. Many Indians are convinced, as Navajo and Hopi elders Catherine Smith and Thomas Banyacya state in the film, that this policy was developed because Indians inhabit lands rich in coal. American Indian Movement leaders, including Clyde Bellecourt, Russell Means, and Bill Means, express their views on how Indians in the United States, though only one percent of the population, can work to gain recognition of their sovereignty.

Even in Bolivia, although the majority of people are Indians, they have not achieved political and economic equality. However, membership in Bolivia's trade unions is predominantly Indian and the most prominent union leader, Pinero Flores, is Indian. He emphasizes the importance of the union movement to give Indians the power to voice their concerns and to have a political leadership that represents their interests. Concluding with an international conference on racism at Geneva, Switzerland, attended by native leaders, the film emphasizes the political advantages for indigenous peoples to work together to gain international recognition for their rights.

HOPI: SONGS OF THE FOURTH WORLD
1983, 58 min. Producer/director: Pat Ferrero. Associate producer: Pat Burke. Camera: James Culp and Emiko Omori. Sound: Tim Metzger, Nelson Stoll, Steve Powell. Editor: Jennifer Chinlund. Narrator: Ronnie Gilbert. 16mm, ¾" vt. Color. Dist.: New Day.

HOPI: SONGS OF THE FOURTH WORLD presents many facets of the present-day life of the Hopi tribe, whose ancient spiritual traditions remain deeply integrated with daily life. The film opens with a brief history stressing the antiquity of Hopi life. The remainder of the film focuses on Hopi philosophy and history, and the resilience of traditional practices.

The production, beautifully filmed, provides vivid impressions of aspects of life in the villages. An artist in his studio, a ritual leader marking solstitial readings on a wall calendar, a young child in front of the television, a family feast, and people harvesting together are shown, a reminder that contemporary Hopi life continues customs and values rooted in the past.

Some people, such as Emory Sekaquaptewa, a university professor, provide a comparison of Hopi with non-Hopi values. His mother, Helen Sekaquaptewa, tells the history of Hopi contacts with the white world that she and her family have experienced and shows a group of young girls a traditional game. The filmmaker was struck by the place of art in Hopi daily life. Several artists, including the renowned painter Fred Kabotie, contribute their views to the film's vision of the Hopi Way.

The cycle of marriage and family, with its contemporary contributions from men and women, is closely connected to the seasonal cycle of growing corn. For the Hopi, corn is a female essence. The film explores this as a metaphor for the significance of women's roles in the society. While no longer the main link it once was to the Hopi people's physical survival, corn is still essential for their cultural and spiritual survival — the Hopi Way which says, "We are corn."

Because of what many Hopis feel has been an abuse of their privacy by photography, the villages usually give outsiders only limited access to film there. This fact underscores Ferrero's achievement in producing a work of such breadth, based on careful research and frequent opportunities for the community to view the work-in-progress and comment on its accuracy. An excellent study guide is available from the distributor. Ferrero has also produced a videotape, PIKI: THE HOPI WAY (for description see Volume I, p. 94).

HOPIIT

1984, 15 min. Producer/director/camera: Victor Masayesva, Jr. Sound: Roy Masayesva and Fred Honhongva. Production assistants: Elwin Kooyahoema and Willis Monongya. Narrators: Ross Macaya and Victor Masayesva, Sr. ¾" vt, ½" vt. Color. Dist.: IS Productions.

Since 1982 an all-Hopi company, headed by award-winning videomaker and photographer Victor Masayesva, Jr., has produced footage for broadcast, and videotapes for diverse art projects and Native American groups. In addition Masayesva has produced experimental videotapes at Hopi.

HOPIIT gives an impressionistic view of a year in the Hopi community. With an absence of explanatory narration, ordinary scenes of Hopi life — a spirited horse, children playing in the snow, peach blossoms during spring thaw, older women weaving baskets, blue corn stored in huge stacks like cords of wood — seem extraordinary. Selected in this way, and beautifully filmed, each moment is heightened.

Masayesva draws from his experience as a still photographer, filming and editing in short sequences as if making moving photographs. He is interested in extending the experiential range of his audience, and strongly resists the didactic narrative which so closely guides a viewer's experience in typical documentary productions. The more knowledgeable of Hopi the viewer is, the more the tape reveals. But even for viewers who are not Hopi nor are deeply informed about their way of life, HOPIIT is satisfying because it is visually exciting and presents Native American life without cliché.

Another production by Masayesva, focused on a traditional storyteller and his presentation of Hopi history, is ITAM HAKIM, HOPIIT (see description in this volume).

THE HONOUR OF ALL
For description see *Walking With Grandfather.*

HUTEETL: KOYUKON MEMORIAL POTLATCH
1983, 55 min. Producer/director/editor: Curt Madison. Camera: Garry Russell. Sound: Trent McNelly. Narrators: Catherine Attla and Eliza Jones. Produced for the Yukon-Koyukuk School District. Executive producers: Niki McCurry and Joe Cooper. ¾" vt, ½" vt. Color. In English and Koyukon Athabascan with English subtitles. Dist.: KYUK/NAPBC.

An excellent example of contemporary Native American community use of media, this videotape is the first documentary filmed of an Athapascan Indian potlatch in interior Alaska. The formal commemorative gathering and its preparations were taped over a period of eight days on the Koyukuk River at a site about 250 miles northwest of Fairbanks. The families sponsoring it requested photographer and videomaker Madison, who at the time was producing video profiles of native elders as part of a regional curriculum project, to make this record of the event. The potlatch honors two family members killed in a plane crash and formally ends a year-long period of mourning.

The tape contains interesting vignettes and conversations. In advance of the potlatch the family hunts and prepares food, tans hides, and makes gifts for the people who have helped throughout the year of mourning. Two lively old women discuss the videotaping, and reminisce over dances they have seen in former years. Participants arrive and are greeted ritually, and feasting and dancing takes place. A family group visits the cemetery, discussing the history of those who are buried there.

The videotape serves not only as a visual record of an important event, the participants feel that it can also play a role in preserving the practice of potlatch. At the time of the plane crash one other Koyukon person was killed and his village no longer remembered the ceremonial observances. This motivated people to be filmed and to explain what they are doing.

The tape also provides a means of addressing another concern of the Koyukon. As preparations for the potlatch feast proceed, people speak of being Alaska natives in terms of the close relationship between traditional Koyukon ways of life and an adequate land base in the present and future. In ceremonial speeches, people examine their culture's values and exhort people to preserve them, stressing the social and spiritual importance of subsistence hunting.

The videomaker skillfully communicates a feeling for Koyukon life. Following the sequence of the event, the videotape, in accordance with Koyukon tradition, allows the viewer to learn by experiencing it, rather than through direct narration. Madison has filmed portraits of three community leaders in KOYUKON REGIONAL PROFILES (for information contact FVC-MAI). In SONGS IN MINTO LIFE he documents how Athapascan elders compose and sing traditional and new songs (see description in this volume).

I KNOW WHO I AM
1979, 28 min. Producer: Sandra Sunrising Osawa. Camera: Yasu Osawa. Sound: Walter Bradley. Produced for KSTW-TV, Seattle. Executive producer: Terry Tafoya. ¾" vt. Color. Dist.: Upstream.

This work by a Makah independent videomaker focuses on cultural values important to Indian tribes of the Pacific coast and was shot on the Makah, Puyallup, and Nisqually reservations. Indian identity is seen as grounded in the life of the family and in its roles of mutual care and the passing on of traditions. Most of the scenes concentrate on women of various ages and their contributions to the survival of Indian traditions.

The program opens with Makah grandmothers singing lullabies for a newborn baby. When gifts are given in the name of the baby to the adults present, the program identifies this as the baby's first lesson in the value of respect for elders. As the Muzzie family practices the traditional Makah songs and dances which, as a family, it has a right to perform, the tape stresses the potential for gaining self-knowledge by participating in family events and learning the family's history.

Osawa interviews several people concerned about the loss of Native American identity and rights. Puyallup leader Ramona Bennett, who helped draft new laws resulting in the national Indian Child Welfare Act, describes the practice of adoption by non-Indians as a kind of genocide. A teacher is interviewed who works at a school on the Nisqually reservation to teach native skills and values to children. Maisel Bridges and his two daughters speak of their participation in the struggle for their tribe's fishing rights. All vignettes are focused on the positive value of Indians' assertion of their traditions and rights. Ultimately, the program shows that to "know who I am" as an Indian is a goal crucial to the continued survival of native peoples and their communities.

I'D RATHER BE POWWOWING

1983, 30 min. Producer: George P. Horse Capture. Director: Larry Littlebird. Sound: Larry Cesspooch. Produced by WNET-TV, New York, for the series Matters of Life or Death. *Executive producer: Carol Brandenberg. 16mm. Color. Dist.: Buffalo Bill.*

Produced for public television entirely by Native Americans, this film presents an unstereotyped portrait of a contemporary Indian and explores the values that are central to his identity. Al Chandler, a senior technical representative for a large corporation, is a Gros Ventre from the Fort Berthold Indian Reservation in North Dakota. Growing up in poverty, he followed his grandfather's advice to get an education and make a good living. In many ways his life is indistinguishable from the middle-class American ideal.

Despite his participation in the economic mainstream which exists off the reservation, Chandler observes Indian traditions by frequently taking part in powwows. The film follows him and his son as they travel to a powwow celebration at the Rocky Boys Reservation near Havre, Montana. During scenes which capture the spirit of the powwow—warm greetings exchanged with friends, preparing food, assembling dance regalia, and dancing—Chandler explains some of its traditional background and meaning.

Even though powwows are generally recognized as American Indian celebrations, misconceptions about their significance to participants reflect the society's general ignorance about most aspects of contemporary Native American life. Chandler describes gathering with other Indian people and powwow dancing both as a kind of home-coming and as an activity of spiritual significance. Beautifully filmed, showing the friendship and pleasure the powwow brings, I'D RATHER BE POWWOWING provides an upbeat view of the life of Indians in the United States today.

IN OUR LANGUAGE

1982, 6 min. Producer/narrator: Edgar Heap of Birds. Camera: Dieter Froese. Editor: Kay Hines Froese. ¾" vt, ½" vt. Color. In English and Cheyenne. Dist.: Edgar Heap of Birds.

A conceptual art piece by Cheyenne artist Edgar Heap of Birds was produced on the large outdoors light board at Times Square in 1982 as part of a project sponsored by New York City. This video documentation of the piece, which the artist suggests should be played sequentially at least two times, involves the viewer directly with Native American experience and language.

As the Tsistsistas (Cheyenne) words become part of the viewer's vocabulary, Cheyenne perspectives become part of the viewer's understanding. Although simply produced, the video effectively reverses the sense of "otherness" with which Native Americans are often forced to live.

IN THE BEST INTEREST OF THE CHILD

For description see *Shenandoah Films.*

IN THE FOOTSTEPS OF TAYTACHA

1985, 30 min. Producer/director/camera/writers: Peter Getzels and Harriet Gordon. Sound: Washington Rozas Alvarez and Peter Getzels. Editor: John Cohen. Narrators: Peter Getzels and Peter West. 16mm, ¾" vt. Color. In Quechua and Spanish with English voice-over and narration. Dist.: DER.

This film follows a group of Quechua Indian villagers as they leave their remote community in the Andes of Peru and join thousands of other highlanders on the annual religious pilgrimage to the sacred peaks of Qoyllur Rit'i, the largest and most important pilgrimage in the southern Andes. From the perspective of the villagers, the festival is an elaborate ritual that retraces the escape route of the Andean god Taytacha who fled from the Catholic priests during the conquest and now inhabits the remotest peaks. From the viewpoint of the Catholic Church, however, the site of the ritual is important because of a miracle there in 1780, the same year the Spanish authorities intensified their campaign to suppress a resurgence of native culture and beliefs.

Throughout the festival individual villagers explain what the ritual means to them. The pilgrimage to Taytacha's location is itself a sacred act. Men wear ritual masks according to the amount of their *cargo* (ritual and social responsibilities they have assumed for the pilgrimage for which Taytacha will grant rewards). Participants in the celebration come from all over the region, including Q'eros and Puno. While capturing the pageantry and devotion of Andean music and dance, the film also documents how Indians of the region have synthesized the sometimes conflicting native and Spanish traditions which are their heritage.

INDIAN HIDE TANNING

For description see *Trust for Native American Cultures and Crafts Video.*

INDIAN LEGENDS OF CANADA

1981–83, 26 min. each. Director: Daniel Bertolino. Produced by Via le Monde. 16mm, ¾" vt, ½" vt. Color. Native languages with English or French narration. Dist.: THA-entire series (US and Canada, sales and rentals)/FH-Programs 1–6, titled LEGENDS OF THE INDIAN (US, sales only).

In this 13-part series, legends of Indian peoples of eastern and northern Canada—

Ojibwa, Montaignais, Micmac, Abnaki, and Carrier—are enacted by Indian people of Ontario and Quebec. The legends are filmed well, and care has been taken to provide authentic clothing, housing, and tools of the Indian tribes whose stories are told. The tales, dealing with such themes as love, death, and people's relationship to the natural world, are convincingly portrayed by the largely non-professional native casts. The tribal origin of the tales are given following each description.

THE WINTER WIFE *(1)*

An ambitious hunter must lose his earthly possessions in order to understand what is truly valuable in life. (Ojibwa)

MOOWIS, WHERE ARE YOU MOOWIS? *(2)*

Two young people lose each other through their stubborn pride and jealousy. (Algonquin)

THE RETURN OF THE CHILD *(3)*

After the death of his wife and son, a man struggles to accept the future without them. (Carrier)

THE LEGEND OF CORN *(4)*

The Great Manitou gives the gift of corn to his people. (Ojibwa)

GLOOSCAP *(5)*

Conflict between two spirit twins accounts for the origin of evil in the world. (Abnaki)

THE PATH OF SOULS/THE WORLD BETWEEN/THE PATH OF LIFE *(6)*

Gujek learns to give up his grief for the death of his young bride, in a legend told in three parts. (Ojibwa)

THE WINDIGO *(7)*

The ferocious Windigo spirit punishes a young man for his greed. (Montagnais)

THE INVISIBLE MAN *(8)*

A miraculous young man brings the first rainbow to the people. (Micmac)

THE SPIRIT OF THE DEAD CHIEF *(9)*

A young chief's experience on the Path of Souls teaches him a lesson about pride. (Ojibwa)

PITCHIE THE ROBIN *(10)*

A youth's search for peace through the beauty of music helps explain the origin of the robin. (Ojibwa)

THE MAGIC BOX *(11)*

With the help of a magic box, a young man learns the meaning of love. (Micmac)

MEGMUWESUG, THE ENCHANTING SPIRIT *(12)*

An impish spirit teaches the people that they must always help one another. (Micmac)

PATH WITHOUT END *(13)*

The spirit world plays a trick on a young man who selfishly attempts to possess beauty. (Ojibwa)

INDIAN SELF-RULE: A PROBLEM OF HISTORY

1985, 58 min. Producer: Selma Thomas. Director: Michael Cotsones. Camera: Barry Kirk, R. D. Willis, and Joel Berhow. Stills: Masayuki Dobashi. Sound: Chris Davis, Steve Stauffer, and Eric Williams. Editors: Selma Thomas and Joel Berhow. Narrator: Ted D'armes. Produced for KWSU-TV, Pullman, WA. Executive producer: Susan S. Francko. ¾" vt, ½" vt. Color. Dist.: DER.

After centuries of struggle, the Indians of North America own less than two percent of the land inhabited by their ancestors. INDIAN SELF-RULE presents a historical outline of federal Indian policy, focusing on the question of tribal sovereignty. In this production tribal leaders, Native American historians, and others gather at a 1983 conference to re-evaluate the significance of the Indian Reorganization Act of 1934 and the implications of more recent federal policies.

The allotment of tribal lands to individuals, federally decreed reorganization of Indian tribes, termination of tribal status, and federal relocation programs are discussed. Speakers comment on the difficulty of maintaining cultural identity within a society that views Indians with ambivalence. The production examines the effects of the shifting federal policies imposed on tribes, which the conference has discussed, through on-site investigations at the reservations of the Flathead in Montana, the Navajo in the Southwest, and the Quinault in Washington state.

Unfortunately, this detailed production suffers from a lack of structural coherence. Scenes of tribal locations are not well-identified or integrated with the interviews filmed there. Even so, INDIAN SELF-RULE is worthwhile for its presentation of the Native American perspective, as well as for providing a wealth of material with which to better understand the legal situation of Indian tribes in the United States.

INUGHUIT: THE PEOPLE AT THE NAVEL OF THE EARTH

1985, 85 min. Directors/sound/editors: Staffan Julen and Ylva Julen. Camera: Michael Rosengreen and Staffen Julen. Produced for the Swedish Film Institute. Executive producer: Staffan Julen. Color. 16mm. In Inuktitut and Danish, with English subtitles. Dist.: Cantor.

This beautifully filmed and directed production focuses on the contemporary life of Inughuit, or Polar Eskimos, living in the Thule district in northernmost Greenland. Its distinctive style is marked by extraordinary views of the Arctic environment throughout the seasons and of the people and animals within it. Its evocative score is composed of a mix of traditional music, natural sounds, and cello. The significance of the environment and people's memories of the recent past and of the various effects of the introduction of non-Inuit culture are themes recurring throughout the film.

It follows a year in the life of the community of Qaanaq, basically a trading post until the 1950's when Inuit of the region were resettled there with the building of an American Strategic Air Command base nearby. The film shows community activities, such as a church wedding followed by a feast of traditional Inuit food and lively nontraditional dancing.

INUGHUIT's primary focus is on the recollections and experiences of individual people. Young adults reflect on their own relationships to Inuit traditions and their future expectations. Filmed at a seasonal narwhal hunting camp, an articulate young man speaks of his desire, and right, to live as a hunter like his father and of the importance of subsistence hunting to continued Inughuit survival. "My heart is out there with Nature. I have experienced such a lot with the elders, out hunting."

For the older generation the memory of the culture of their youth is still strong. A grandmother shows a group of children how she tended her stone lamp in the days before electricity, gently answering their questions. The son of the Black explorer Matthew Hensen, who accompanied Commodore Peary on his quest to the North Pole, speaks of his extraordinary father. An elder sings sacred songs, accompanying himself on a dustpan which serves as a tambour drum. "When my father (a shaman) was baptised, he was forced to throw away his songs, but I picked them up in case I might need them."

INUGHUIT is the work of two Swedish independent filmmakers and reflects their appreciation of the culture and people they are documenting. The film, while discussing change, shows that Inughuit culture is strong for the people of Qaanaq and that they are active in synthesising for themselves their own modern way of life. This documentary is poetic, and yet conveys a sense of having portrayed its subject with accuracy and a sure sense of the complex and multifaceted aspects of a contemporary Inuit community.

INUPIAT ESKIMO HEALING

1985, 30 min. Producer: Nellie Moore. Director/camera/editor: Daniel Housberg. Production technicians: Marley Gregg and Linda Lee. Produced by the Northwest Arctic Television Center. Executive producer: Bob Walker. ¾" vt, ½" vt. Color. In English and Inupiaq with English subtitles. Dist.: Northwest Arctic. For additional information see NORTHWEST ARCTIC VIDEO.

INUPIAT ESKIMO HEALING looks at the practice of medicine in northern Alaska today by following several traditional doctors and their patients in three Inupiat villages. The history of medicine and healing techniques used in the past and adapted to the present are documented, as patients are treated. Arthritic pain and injuries to joints and back are treated by *kapi*, or bloodletting, which is discussed from several viewpoints in the film. Care of well babies and other medical needs are attended to in the village clinics. Interviews with two non-native doctors draw a contrast between traditional and Western medicine. The program observes that as medical authorities learn to include Inupiat healers in providing health care, the synthesis of the best of traditional and nontraditional medicine will be developed in rural Alaska.

INUPIAT LEGENDS SERIES

For description see *Northwest Arctic Video.*

ITAM HAKIM, HOPIIT

1984, 60 min. Producer/director/camera: Victor Masayesva, Jr. Sound: Fred Honhongva and Roy Masayesva. Production managers: Madeline Sahneyah and Jennifer Joseph. Produced for ZDF-German Television. ¾" vt, ½" vt. Color. In Hopi or English. Dist.: IS Productions (sales)/Intermedia (rentals).

In this innovative work by Hopi independent videomaker Victor Masayesva and an all-Hopi crew, one of the last members of the tribe's storytelling clan, Ross Macaya, recounts his life story and various epochs in Hopi history. The production consists of visual sequences and frequent close-ups with a narrative track of the elder's tales, natural sounds, and music.

ITAM HAKIM, HOPIIT opens with shots of Macaya's feet in old sneakers, as he goes to fill a bucket with water. Telling of his childhood, the old man describes growing up without a father and his generation's reluctance to participate in the white man's world. He shifts from speaking of his own history to telling the story of the origin of his clan and the emergence of the Hopi from sacred times into this present world. Beautiful vignettes are juxtaposed with his account — red, then blue, corn pouring down from winnowing baskets, canyon cliffs crumbling, and the cool white moon.

The historical past — the Spanish invasion and Pueblo Revolt of 1680 — are evoked in footage using experimental chromatic changes of a mounted conquistador and of Hopi runners today. Macaya's tale concludes with an apocalyptic image of the world out of kilter, represented by scenes of Hopi dances performed in the plaza by adults and children, in regular and speeded-up time. The tape ends with the serene image of two people at work in the fields; according to the Hopi Prophecy, the next world will begin with two good people.

Masayesva has carefully chosen imagery to correspond to the elder's account. Frequently the visuals present a layer of symbols particularly meaningful to a Hopi audience. For example, as the elder tells of the origin of death, the tape shows in close-up a captive eagle. The view of the bird is striking and underscores the serious nature of the tale. Eagles are sacred to the Hopi — they are ceremonially sacrificed and their feathers are used to make prayer sticks. As the tale continues, children are shown listening and acting silly in Macaya's cabin. Here the Hopi audience knows that Maasaw, the god of death, is also associated with unpredictable and foolish events.

In his presentation of the Hopi world from within the culture, Masayesva confronts what he sees as the tyranny of non-Indian approaches to documentation. Although both versions are excellent, viewing ITAM HAKIM, HOPIIT in its original Hopi language is deeply affecting. Its strong, almost iconic, visuals permit audiences to respond on many levels. Here and in other videotapes such as HOPIIT (see description in this volume), Masayesva displays an exceptional sensibility and creates works rich with implications.

JAUNE QUICK-TO-SEE SMITH

1983, 29 min. Producer: Jack Peterson. Director: Anthony Schmitz. Writer: Joy Harjo. Camera: Don Cirillo. Narrator: N. Scott Momaday. Produced by the Native American Public Broadcasting Consortium. Executive producer: Frank Blythe. 16mm, all video formats. Color. Dist.: NAPBC.

One of the American Indian Artists series produced by the Native American Public Broadcasting Consortium, this production is an imaginative introduction to the work and thought of an outstanding contemporary Native American painter. It sensitively conveys Jaune Quick-To-See Smith's personal vision and its relation to her painting. As the film opens, the camera lingers on the artist at work, giving the feeling that the viewer is present in her New Mexico studio, observing her unseen. In her paintings she combines a personal iconography with expressions of her Indian identity. Scenes of the artist's immediate environment and some of the things she cares deeply about — her animals and the land —

are echoed in poetry by Smith and Creek poet Joy Harjo recited as part of the narration.

Interwoven with the film's portrayal of the creative process is the artist's intimate account of her personal and artistic odyssey, told in interviews and in a lively discussion filmed with artist Emmie Lou Whitehorse. Quick-To-See Smith has provided inspiration for an entire generation of younger artists, not only by showing her work nationally, but also by her support of their professional and artistic development.

JOURNEY TO THE SKY: A HISTORY OF THE ALABAMA AND COUSHATTA INDIANS

1982, 53 min. Director/writer/camera: Paul Yeager. Editor: John Snavely. Narrators: Marcellus Bearheart Williams and Robert Symonds. Tribal coordinator: Thomas Sylvestine. Produced by KUHT-TV, Houston. Executive producer: Robert Cozens. 16mm, ¾" vt. Color. Dist.: KUHT/THRC.

This videotape presents the complicated history of two Southeast Indian tribes, told both in the linear fashion of Western television documentaries and in mythic terms by Alabama chief Fulton Battise. "Three boys lived a long time ago . . . They decided to go to the end of the world." Weaving through the tape's narrative segments, this story acts as a metaphor for the tribes' history. The Alabama and Coushatta Indians, allies of the powerful Creek nation, lived in central Alabama until the arrival of the Europeans. Their relations with successive European powers were mixed. When their French allies ceded "their" territory in America to Great Britain, many of the tribes' people left the area and headed west, ultimately settling together in the Big Thicket of eastern Texas.

Settlement in Texas by whites led to the loss of lands and the destruction of the Indians' economic base. The work of missionaries in the nineteenth century, and the loss of government services in the twentieth, have profoundly increased the pressures they face. Now the Alabama and Coushatta, looking to the future, are greatly concerned that their history and culture as native peoples may not survive.

The tape is heavily scripted and visually somewhat static, presenting information in detail. By including a tribal way of telling history, it underscores its basic premise that these two tribes, like many others seen by outsiders as acculturated, still retain their Indian identity.

JUDEA
For description see *Maria Sabina: Mujer Espiritu.*

JUST A SMALL FISHERY
For description see *KYUK Video.*

KAMINURIAK: CARIBOU IN CRISIS
1982–3, 33 programs, 4 to 20 min. each. Produced by the Inuit Broadcasting Corporation and Don Snowden. Sponsored by the Department of Indian and Northern Affairs, Canada. ¾" vt, ½" vt. Color. In Inuktitut and English. Dist.: IBC.

For the Inuit of Canada's northern barren lands the great caribou herds were traditionally the core of subsistence. Though most Inuit of this region now live in settlements and use modern products and technologies, subsistence hunting is still important. In recent years change has affected both the ecological and cultural practices in the North. The caribou herds have been decreasing; of particular concern is the Kaminuriak Herd, which ranges along the southwestern shore of Hudson Bay in the Northwest Territories. Opinions differ widely as to why this is happening.

The view shared by many Inuit hunters and their wives is that biologists studying the herd deprecate their views and the knowledge accumulated through generations of hunting. They feel the scientists do not adequately assess the damage done to the herds by modern development and mining. The Inuit also describe traditional ways of hunting and using the products of the caribou as they have practiced them in the past and present.

Biologists and game management personnel believe overhunting by the Keewatin Inuit has caused herd reduction. They are concerned that the Inuit are unwilling to acknowledge the impact of their use of modern hunting technology. To improve understanding, it was decided to use video to document the conflicting views; thirty-three interviews were filmed by the Inuit Broadcasting Corporation. By presenting both sides of the issue and contrasting approaches to wildlife management, KAMINURIAK shows the problem's complexity and the perspectives of the people most involved with it.

The Inuit Broadcasting Corporation (IBC) is a Native American media organization producing programs in Inuktitut and in English primarily for broadcast in the Arctic over the Canadian Broadcasting Corporation's Northern Television service. Its origins in a pioneering television project under the direction of the Inuit Tapirisat of Canada and funded by the Canadian government in the late 1970's are documented in MAGIC IN THE SKY (see description in this volume and p. 134 in Volume I).

Current productions of IBC include docu-dramas on alcohol abuse and family problems and documentaries of contemporary Inuit communities. Contact IBC (see distributors index) for descriptions of the individual programs in KAMINURIAK and for a complete listing of all other productions in distribution.

KEEPERS OF THE FOREST

1985, 28 min. Producer/director/editor: Norman Lippman. Writers: Norman Lippman and Eric Von Schrader. Camera: Norman Lippman, Greig Forrest, Randy Freeman, and Lois Gilliam. Sound: Norman Lippman, Clayton Marlow, and Richard Alderson. Narrators: Donna Michaels Race and Ollie Raymond. Dist.: Lippman.

KEEPERS OF THE FOREST discusses the vital importance of tropical rainforests to the global ecology. Through narration and interviews with ecologists and botanists it examines the implications of the deforestation now taking place on a vast scale worldwide. It focuses on the Lacandon Maya of Naha in Chiapas, Mexico, who inhabit the last tropical rainforest of significant size in North America, examining their agricultural techniques as a model for sustaining the natural ecology.

The production sketches out conditions leading to deforestation there, including industrial logging and the movement of mestizo and highland Maya peasants who are being encouraged to settle in forest areas and clear the land for agriculture. Because they are unfamiliar with a rainforest ecosystem, the land is quickly degraded and abandoned, generally to be succeeded by cattle raising.

By contrast, Lacandon Maya agriculture is ecologically sophisticated and makes a complex fit with the fragile balance of the rainforest. Lacandon elders explain the Maya system which results in high yields without causing damage to the ecosystem. The production documents their practice of multi-cropping, producing more than eighty farm and garden foods. It also touches on the sacred cosmology of the Lacandon Maya that underlies their use of the environment.

KLEENA

1981, 20 min. Director/camera: H. Leslie Smith. Writer: Dann Firehouse. Narrator for Peter Knox's account: Peter Scow. 16mm. Color. Dist.: CFDW.

A small group of Kwakiutl Indians, organized by Peter Knox, the grandson of famed carver Mungo Martin, sets out from their community at Alert Bay to participate in a traditional fishing activity. They travel to hereditary fishing grounds at the head of Knight Inlet to net the oil-rich eulachon fish, and to render the oil, called *kleena*. It is used in cooking, in preserving fish, and as a feast food for potlatches.

The narration gives general economic and social facts related to kleena. It also tells the story of the legendary origin of eulachon and its importance to the Kwakiutl. Alternating with this narrative, Peter Knox describes the trip as a personal experience, telling how a successful journey to obtain kleena can "make good" the fisherman's name. He speaks of his family and clan history and gives a running commentary both on the trip and on the many steps necessary in the process of producing the eulachon oil.

KOYUKON REGIONAL PROFILES

For description see *Huteetl: Koyukon Memorial Potlatch.*

KYUK VIDEO

Executive producer: John A. McDonald. All video formats. Color. In Yup'ik or English. Dist.: KYUK.

Located in Bethel, Alaska, KYUK-TV, begun in 1972, has produced works on the lifestyles and native culture of the Yukon-Kuskokwim Delta, both for local broadcast and for the general public. It produces radio and television programs in both English and Yup'ik.

KYUK's video production department has made over thirty documentaries. The themes of the programs are consistently interesting, but vary in style and production values. They focus on the Yup'ik Eskimo way of life and the people's viewpoints on contemporary events and the continuation of their cultural traditions. The station has provided opportunities for community members to be involved as production consultants and spokesmen in the programs and also has employed native producers, cinematographers, narrators, and on-camera interviewers. For a complete listing of KYUK video programs, contact the distributor. Several outstanding KYUK productions are described under their individual titles:

EYES OF THE SPIRIT
FROM HAND TO HAND: BETHEL NATIVE ARTIST PROFILES
A MATTER OF TRUST
THEY NEVER ASKED OUR FATHERS
YUPIIT YURARYARAIT/A DANCING PEOPLE

For a complete listing of other productions contact the distributor. Some of these include:

JUST A SMALL FISHERY

1984, 28 min. Producers· Mike Martz and Richard Goldstein.

This production presents the efforts of three western Bering Sea coastal communities to establish a locally controlled commercial herring fishery.

OLD DANCES, NEW DANCERS

1984, 29 min. Producer: Mike Martz.

This program documents the first Young People's Eskimo Dance Awareness Festival organized in Chevak, Alaska, intended to revitalize traditional dancing.

PARLEZ-VOUS YUP'IK?

1985, 60 min. Producer: John A. McDonald.

KYUK's crew follows a Yup'ik theater group from Toksook Bay, Alaska, as they travel to the Theater of Nations Festival in Nancy, France, and to LaMama Playhouse, one of the New York's most celebrated avant-garde theaters. A videotape of YUP'IK ANTIGONE, their version of Sophocles' play performed in Yup'ik, is also available from KYUK.

PEOPLE OF KASHUNUK

1983, 28 min. Producer: Bill Sharpsteen.

A family portrait filmed in the village of Chevak, this program examines traditional culture and change in the twentieth century.

LAKOTA QUILLWORK: ART AND LEGEND

1985, 27 min. Producer/director/editor: H. Jane Nauman. Camera: Charles Nauman. Narrators: Alice Blue Legs and H. Jane Nauman. 16mm, ¾" vt, ½" vt. Color. In English and Lakota. Dist.: OneWest.

Using special effects, LAKOTA QUILLWORK opens with an account, from mythic times, of the origin of quillwork as a gift from Double Woman, with whom quillworkers maintained a special relationship through dreams. The production then proceeds to show two well-known contemporary quillworkers, Flossie New Holy Bear Robe and Alice New Holy Blue Legs. They re-enact a scene as it might have appeared 150 years ago when great honors and sacred obligations were accorded the women who made major articles such as buffalo robes. Their buffalo hide tipi is arranged with numerous quilled furnishings, clothing, and objects of daily use. As they demonstrate sewn and wrapped quilling, they explain the process in Lakota, with English translation added.

The location of the documentary shifts to the present-day home of Alice New Holy Blue Legs in the Grass Creek community on the Pine Ridge Reservation in South Dakota. Recently honored by a National Endowment for the Arts folk arts award, the artist took up the quillwork she had learned as a girl when she realized it had almost become a lost art among her people. Now members of her family continue the tradition. The film shows their work, beginning with the porcupine hunt, cleaning and sorting quills by size, dyeing them, and making quilled jewelry and dance regalia. As one of the only productions to document the meaning and process of this traditional art, LAKOTA QUILLWORK makes a valuable addition to the films available on Native American arts and processes.

LENAPE: THE ORIGINAL PEOPLE

1986, 22 min. Producer/director/editor: Thomas Agnello. Camera: Alberto Bader. Sound: Jack O'Neall. Resource coordinator: David Oestreicher. 16mm, ¾" vt, ½" vt. Dist.: Agnello.

The Delaware, or Lenape, lived originally in parts of New Jersey, eastern Pennsylvania, and northern Delaware. Their hold on their lands was under great pressure from the seventeenth century on, and gradually almost all the tribe moved or were pushed westward. Delaware descendants today live in Oklahoma and on the Six Nations Reserve in Ontario, as well as New Jersey and the other eastern states.

Because the people were scattered and integrated into the larger established communities of the other tribes with whom they settled, much of Delaware tradition has been lost. This film, while briefly sketching Delaware history, is focused on two elders living in Dewey, Oklahoma, who retain the language and knowledge of old customs and beliefs. Edward Thompson describes his participation in a Big House Ceremony in 1924, the last time this important ceremony was held. He speaks with regret of past traditions and the young people who no longer seem to have an interest in continuing them.

Thompson's sister, Nora Thompson Dean, was also filmed shortly before her death. Known as Touching Leaves Woman, she was highly respected for her efforts to keep Delaware heritage alive and to preserve a record of its traditions. In this film she shares memories of her mother, empowered by a vision to be a name giver, and tells a legend about Rabbit. Invited to lecture in New Jersey in 1970, she movingly describes seeing the land of her ancestors for the first time, and muses on the future of the Delaware and the cultural loss they have sustained. Scenes of the first reunion of Lenape from all parts of the United States and Canada, held in 1983, are included.

LETTER FROM AN APACHE

1983, 12 min. Producer/writer/animator: Barbara Wilk. Camera: Animus Films. Narrator: Fred Hellerman. 16mm, ¾" vt, ½" vt. Color animation. Dist.: Barr/Centre.

This animated film is an imaginative presentation of the remarkable experiences of a Yavapai Indian (not Apache) of the early twentieth century. The narration is adapted from a letter written by Carlos Montezuma, M.D., known as Wassajah, to Frederick W. Hodge to provide autobiographical information for the 1907 *Handbook of American Indians*. Montezuma was witness to a period of vast changes in Indian life in the Southwest, including a policy put into effect to place Indian groups on reservations.

Unrest in the region during the latter quarter of the nineteenth century was reflected in the fact that his people had taken refuge with a band of Chiricahua Apache. As a young boy, he was seized by marauders and bought or adopted by a white man. Taken to Chicago, he became a doctor and practiced and taught medicine. Although not discussed in this film, Montezuma was also an Indian lecturer and newsletter editor, convinced that Indians should integrate themselves into the American society of the day to obtain its privileges and rights.

The animation for LETTER FROM AN APACHE is based on the drawing style of Indian "ledger book" artists held in captivity during the period of forced reservation settlement in the late nineteenth century. It provides a moving visualization for the story of historical and personal upheavals that characterized the youth of this eminent Native American. Other animations by Wilk include EMERGENCE (see description this volume) and QUEEN VICTORIA AND THE INDIANS, based on a first-person observation by the painter and showman George Catlin of a group of Ojibwa Indians performing in his show in London (Dist.: Barr/Centre).

LIVING TRADITIONS: FIVE INDIAN WOMEN ARTISTS

1984, 27 min. Producer/director/editors: Fran Belvin, Denise Mayotte, and Kathee Prokop. Camera: Fran Belvin, Kathee Prokop, Michael Rivard, and Kathy Seltzer. Sound: Dave Adams. Narrator: Sherry Wilson. Original music: Twilight Spirit Duo. Produced by Womanswork and Iris Video. ¾" vt, ½" vt. Color. Dist.: Intermedia.

This videotape recognizes the achievements of Indian women artists, whose work is often "art that is meant to be used." It profiles five women of different ages and tribal affiliations — Ojibwa, Cree, Dakota Sioux, and Yankton-Sisseton Sioux — who live and work in Minnesota. Interviews with the artists demonstrate that Native American women play an essential role in preserving their cultures in the face of pressures to relinquish their traditions and identity.

The production shows these artists strongly reflecting Indian tradition. Elizabeth Kingbird concentrates on sewing jingle dresses and making other articles of dance regalia for her family. Terry Brightnose produces beautiful quill- and beadwork. Josie Ryan exhibits traditional beadwork and baskets and teaches these skills at Bemidji State University. Each speaks with pride about making work that is significant to their families' Indian identity and economic survival.

Even when they have adopted European forms and materials, such as the star quilts sewn by Edith Sigana, Indian tradition and aesthetics are evoked. The youngest artist interviewed, Cynthia Holmes, works as a fashion designer whose creations blend traditional and contemporary styles and materials. She also teaches art at the Native American alternative school, the Red School House. At the conclusion of the tape she muses on the survival of Indian tradition and urges her audience, "Don't forget it — if you do your own children will."

THE LONGEST TRAIL

1985, 58 min. Producer: Alan Lomax. Directors: Alan Lomax and Forrestine Paulay. Editor: Molly Smollett with Donna Marino. 16mm, ¾" vt, ½" vt (VHS, Beta). Color. Dist.: UCEMC.

The hallmark of Lomax and Paulay's films, produced to demonstrate the relationship between dance style and culture, has been their use of extraordinary selections of film footage. In THE LONGEST TRAIL, they focus on Native America to show that patterns of movement link the dances of Indians and Inuit from the Arctic Circle to Tierra del Fuego into one tradition. The film also seeks to demonstrate a connection between these cultures and indigenous cultures in Siberia.

This is a theoretical film, most appropriate for academic use. However, many audiences will be very interested in the selections of dances included here from more than fifty groups, as well as footage of shamanism, drama, ritual, work, and the making of artifacts. Among the Native American cultures represented in the film clips are Pomo, Mesquakie, Haida, Kwakiutl, Navajo, Blackfeet, Apache, Hopi, Tarahumara, Huichol, Totonac, Yucatec Maya, Cuna, Panare, Karaja, Quechua, Ona, and Inuit, as well as the Ainu of Japan, and Mansi and Khanty of Siberia. A teacher's guide is available from the distributor.

LOST IN TIME

1985, 57 min. Producers: Bruce G. Kuerten and Maryanne G. Culpepper. Production designer: J. Anderson Luster. Art director: John Gullatte. Camera: Bobby Chandler, Al Colley, Cedron Wynn. Music: William Michael Davis. Narrator: Dennis King. Consultant: Joseph O. Vogel. Produced by Auburn Television. ¾" vt, ½" vt. Color. Dist.: Auburn.

Twelve thousand years ago early Indian cultures lived in the rich forest of the Tennessee Valley. Visiting sites and interviewing scholars, LOST IN TIME observes the work of archeologists in the area. It also traces the history of the early native peoples whose way of life has been given a detailed description by such scholarly efforts. The tape describes American prehistory beginning with the migration of Paleolithic hunters into the New World over the Bering land bridge. It briefly discusses the changes of Indian culture leading to the complex settled lifestyle of the Indians who built the great mounds of the Black Warrior River Valley in Alabama. The program presents information about early Indian life through re-enactments which focus on artifacts and their use.

LOST IN TIME is a welcome addition to productions available on archeology and Native American prehistory in the Southeast. Ending with questions about why these cultures disappeared, the program does not discuss the existence of historically known and contemporary tribes of the region. However, it successfully heightens the viewer's interest in the fascinating cultural tradition of Alabama's earliest inhabitants.

MAGIC IN THE SKY

1980–81, 57 min. Producers: Peter Raymont and Arthur Hammond. Director/writer: Peter Raymont. Camera: Ian Elkin and Martin Duckworth. Sound: Leon Johnson, Aerlyn Weissman, Claude Beaugrand, and Richard Nichol. Editor: Michael Fuller. Translator: Sarah Pitseolak. Narrator: Michael Kane. Research consultant: Kenneth G. O'Bryan. Produced for the National Film Board of Canada by Investigative Productions. 16mm ¾" vt. Color. Dist.: Karol Media (US Rentals)/NFBC (US sales). In Canada, contact local NFBC offices.

MAGIC IN THE SKY is concerned with the impact of television in the Canadian Arctic. Since 1972 the Canadian Broadcasting Corporation (CBC) has beamed commercial programming by satellite into most villages in the Arctic for eighteen hours a day. Popular American and Canadian television shows, including soap operas, action dramas, and advertisements, expose the audience to unfamiliar views of violence and consumerism. As Inuit leader John Amagoalik says, the effect of television has been drastic. It competes with community activities and, located in the home, becomes an English-language invader of the last refuge of the Inuktitut language. But, he continues, television is also potentially of great use to the Inuit in a time of rapid change.

The film documents efforts by two Inuit media organizations to use television for their own purposes. On the Arctic coast of Quebec, which had chosen to receive no CBC broadcasts, Tagramiut Nipingat Inc. (TNI) was formed to cover community political meetings and to re-edit and narrate world news for broadcast to its Inuit audience.

In 1980, after several years of lobbying, the Inuit Tapirisat of Canada was granted access to a CBC satellite channel, creating Inukshuk, an experimental television network to provide regionally originated programs and to offset the "southern" programming CBC provides. Six communities across the central and western Arctic became the sites for production and reception of programs. One of these, Igloolik, had no television prior to Inukshuk. The film documents community life without television, and covers a referendum held to decide whether to accept CBC broadcasting.

Working with professional trainers, the Inukshuk staff is shown in studios at Frobisher Bay, Baker Lake, and Eskimo Point and on location. A performance of throat singing and interviews with hunters are filmed. On Baffin Island, another production center, a caribou hunt is both filmed and described by one of the hunters. To observe major studio techniques, three producers go to New York City, filming themselves with the stars of a program popular in the Arctic, *The Edge of Night*, and watching the televising of the Stanley Cup finals. Upon their return the new network is launched, broadcasting news and local programming in Inuktitut.

The Inukshuk project was time-limited and after six months open access to the satellite was no longer made available by CBC. It had successfully demonstrated, however, that an audience for Inuit programs and a professional staff to produce them were there. From it developed the Inuit Broadcasting Corporation (IBC) which now produces and broadcasts by satellite five and half hours a week of original programming on the CBC Northern Television band.

MAGIC IN THE SKY skillfully examines the possibilities and problems inherent in native participation in television. Its director, Peter Raymont, has produced other films of contemporary Inuit life and the impact of media and "southern" culture. SIKSILARMIUT and ANIMATIONS FROM CAPE DORSET (both distributed by NFBC) show an Inuit film animation workshop and the students' productions. ARCTIC SPIRITS is concerned with fundamentalist evangelism in the North (see description in this volume). For more information about IBC and its productions see the description of KAMINURIAK — CARIBOU IN CRISIS (in this volume).

MAGIC WINDOWS

1981, 58 min. Producer: Manuel Arango. Directors: Hugh and Suzanne Johnston. Sound: Claire Johnston and Alejandro Salvida. Narrator: Pootase Woodford. 16mm, ¾" vt. Color. In English or Spanish, Dist.: Johnston.

While focusing on the life of an artist, MAGIC WINDOWS is also a portrait of the Nahuatl-speaking village of San Agustin, located in the Sierra Madre Mountains in the Mexican state of Guerrero. The subject of the film is folk artist Abraham Mauricio Salazar who makes intricate drawings on *amate* paper, which is made from fig bark. The film opens with Salazar journeying twelve hours from home to sell his work in the market at Tepotzlan. As it proceeds, it documents his work and life, including the everyday activities which are the inspiration for his drawings.

Agriculture figures in Salazar's work since he, like the other villagers, is a farmer. MAGIC WINDOWS portrays the cycle of growing corn — tilling and planting the fields, ritual prayer and seasonal changes that bring rain, and the ripening and harvesting of the crops. The theme of harvest is counterpointed by a description of the sadness of death, reflected in Salazar's drawings, and by a view of the celebration of the feast of Todos Santos. The film concludes with an homage to Salazar and the love of life manifested in his art.

A scripted voice-over narration is meant to represent the interior thoughts of the artist, but without any direct commentary from Salazar it is unclear how well it actually represents him. However, it is a well-filmed and sympathetic portrayal of an Indian village on the edge of change and offers audiences a rare view of the background of a Mexican folk art which is seen in markets far removed from its region of origin.

MAKE MY PEOPLE LIVE: THE CRISIS IN INDIAN HEALTH CARE

1984, 60 min. Producer/director/writer: Linda Harrar. Associate producer: Barbara Costa. Camera: Hillyard J. Brown. Sound: Robert Eber, John Osborne, and Bob Marts. Editor: Eric A. Neudel. Narrator: Lee Grant. Produced by WGBH-TV, Boston, for the series NOVA. Executive producer: John Mansfield. 16mm (sales only), ¾" vt (sales and rentals). Color. Dist.: TLV.

As the Indian Health Care Improvement Act (IHCIA) was coming up for renewal in the spring of 1984, the public television series NOVA aired this informative program on Indian health care in the United States. Much information little known by many non-Indians is given, including the explanation that federal obligations to Indian tribes, such as the provision of free health care, are specified in treaties and other agreements as part of the compensation for lands that were ceded by the tribes. The Federal Indian Health Service provides Native Americans with health care. Although this agency has helped to improve their physical health, its services remain inadequate to cope with either the amount of serious disease and infant mortality faced by Native Americans or with illnesses stemming from the poverty and demoralization that exist in many reservations and native communities.

As this production shows, the quality of medical programs and the amount of community control varies. Sites visited range from the impoverished Rosebud Sioux Reservation with its half-condemned Indian Health Service hospital, to the Tlingit villages of Alaska, where Indian health aides carry out medical requirements under physicians' guidance and training. At the Navajo Nation, Navajo aides assist with visits to remote households where many of the older people speak only their own language. Shown practicing medicine in their own communities are Dr. Lucy Reifel (Lakota) and Dr. Dan Bowen (Creek). Staffing medical programs with Indian health workers helps to ensure greater success, probably because of the fact that they share a world view with their patients that promotes healing.

The Creek Nation of Oklahoma, which operates the only hospital facility for Indians and non-Indians in its area, provides an example of a tribe responding to the Indian Self-Determination Act by contracting with the federal government to run its own health facilities. The act, passed in 1975, has encouraged tribes, with government financial support, to control enterprises in their own communities. The documentary also investigates the state of health care for

Indians who have relocated to cities; over half of America's native population now live in urban centers and are served by clinics funded under the IHCIA.

Despite the pressing needs that this film shows so effectively, this act was not renewed in 1984, with only interim funds being made available until Congress acts on the legislation. MAKE MY PEOPLE LIVE is well-researched, produced, and filmed. By showing details of Native American life in four vastly different regions and discussing legislative and other issues, it provides an outstanding introduction not only to health concerns but also to contemporary life of Native Americans across the country.

MAKE PRAYERS TO THE RAVEN

Producer/camera/editor: Mark Badger. Writer/associate producer: Richard K. Nelson. Sound/ associate producer: Wayne Attla. Narrator: Barry Lopez. Music: John Luther Adams. Produced by KUAC-TV, University of Alaska, Fairbanks. Executive Producer: Chuck McConnell. All video formats. Color. Dist.: KUAC.

This public television series introduces the lifeways and traditions of interior Alaska's Koyukon Indians. Focusing on their relationship to the land, it explores the spiritual beliefs which pervade all aspects of subsistence for traditional Koyukon. Included in the filming were four of the eleven Koyukon communities — Alatna, Allakaket, Hughes, and Huslia — located just below the Arctic Circle in the Koyukon River Valley. MAKE PRAYERS TO THE RAVEN was produced with the Tleeyagga Hut'aaninh Committee, made up of representatives from the four villages, which made decisions about each program's content. For information about a study guide for use in secondary schools contact the distributor.

THE PASSAGES OF GIFTS (1)

Through narration and commentary by villagers the Koyukon world view and ideas about the relationship between humans and the natural world are described. How these beliefs are put into practice in subsistence pursuits is examined in scenes of hunting and trapping.

THE BIBLE AND THE DISTANT TIME (2)

Christianity has largely been adopted in Koyukon villages. In an interview an elder discusses the ancient set of principles and practices, *hutlanee*, that teach the proper conduct toward nature. She tells how she has been able to reconcile Koyukons beliefs, preserved in stories of the "distant time", with a Christian view. However, some aspects of non-native society cause conflicts, especially for the young. The production shows a memorial gathering held for a young victim of alcoholism. The ceremony, combining both traditional Koyukon and Christian customs, helps breach the loss felt by the community.

THE FOREST OF EYES (3)

Filmed at summer fish camp on the Koyukon River, a family net fishes to obtain its year's supply of salmon. Family members discuss their traditional way, in which no part of the fish is wasted and no more than can be processed in a day are caught. Voice-over narration adds detail about Koyukon concepts of the relationship between man and fish.

GRANDPA JOE'S COUNTRY (4)

Joe Beetus, whose family moved to the Koyukon River Valley in birch bark canoes sixty-five years ago, is a living link with the Koyukon past. Filmed during a fall moose hunt, he shares his knowledge of traditional hunting and his thoughts about living on the land.

THE LIFE IN THE BEAR (5)

For the Koyukon, few spirits in nature have the power of the black bear. Of all the animals hunted probably none requires more special acts of respect or has as many restrictions on its pursuit and handling after being killed. The bear hunt is essentially a sacred pursuit and its documentation on film is an unusual event. The videotape shows the reverence with which the hunt is carried out and some of its ceremonial aspects.

MARA'ACAME

For description see *Mexico Indigena Series.*

MARIA SABINA: MUJER ESPIRITU

1979, 80 min. Director/camera: Nicolas Echevarría. Writer: Alvaro Estrada. Editor: Saul Aupart. Music: Mario Lavista. Produced by the Centro de Produccion de Cortometraje, Mexico. 35mm. Color. In Mazatec with English, French, or Spanish translation and narration. Dist.: Centro de Produccion.

Lyrically filmed, this work depicts Maria Sabina, a Mazatec shaman and healer living in Huautla, in the mountains near Oaxaca, Mexico. Using hallucinogenic mushrooms to do "surgery on the soul," she practices a timeless healing art. The film is transcendant in tone, shot whenever possible by natural light to convey the filmmaker's sense of the shaman's holiness. It focuses on ritual healing— candles, incense, chants, hallucinogenic mushrooms, and the interaction between Maria Sabina and her patient.

  The film provides an evocative experience of shamanic healing. The text is synthesized from Maria Sabina's own conversation and chants to offer a first-person narrative which is poetic in its utterance. Ceremonials in Mazatec are not explained, but subtitles translate the words spoken or sung. By presenting ritual as an aesthetic experience, Echevarría has experimented with how film can convey to a non-native audience what will remain to them the mystery of traditional practices. However, a consideration of ceremony as a visual event isolates its performance from the meaning it holds for its participants.

  As in other films by Echevarría, the camera serves to capture the ritual of gesture and the rhythm of ritual, and to circumvent what the filmmaker sees as the intrusions of explanatory narrative. He has stated that he is "obsessed with things that have no rational explanation." He has documented Indian peasant musicians in POETAS CAMPESINOS (Popoluca) and aspects of other Indian religious observances in northern Mexico, including Easter rituals in JUDEA (Cora) and TESHUINADA (Tarahumara) and peyote rituals in HIKURI-TAME (Huichol). For further information contact Echevarría (see distributors index).

MASHPEE

1985, 50 min. or 28 min. Producer/director/writer/editors: Maureen McNamara and Mark Gunning. Camera: Mark Gunning, ¾" vt, ½" vt. Color. Dist: McNamara.

The problem facing Indian communities which pursue land claims in the absence of treaties is dramatically illustrated in the case of the Mashpee Wampanoags. They have been engaged in a legal battle for the recognition of ownership of lands in and around the town of Mashpee, Massachusetts, since 1976. Although court hearings have not brought them satisfaction, this investigation gives the complex background of the controversy, and suggests that in different circumstances the outcome might have been different.

It is an ironic story, as the Mashpee historically dwelt in peace side by side with outsiders who came to inhabit their area and accepted many aspects of non-Indian culture. However, 19th-century rulings of the Massachusetts legislature stripped them of tribal status and sixteen thousand acres of land and laid the grounds for the current dispute. The issue of the Mashpees' control of lands is complicated by their claim's dependence on proof of tribal status, an issue well-covered in the longer version, and by the development of a rapidly growing summer community in the town of Mashpee.

In interviews Mashpee leaders, real estate developers, historians, legal experts, and the trial lawyers present their sides of the story. At the conclusion of the video, one Mashpee leader speaks emphatically about his Indian identity. "My forefathers were put here as Mashpee Wampanoags . . . I'm not less Indian because I teach school, or own a business." The Mashpee are pursuing their case, finding that in the 1980's they want to insist more forcefully on a recognition of their tribal identity, now long overdue. In 1981 they filed another suit, dismissed by the same judge who had ruled against them earlier, and the case is now under appeal.

A MATTER OF TRUST

1983, 28 min. Producer/writer/editor/host: Bill Sharpsteen. Camera: Alexie Isaac, Mike Martz, Corlene Rose, and Bill Sharpsteen. Narrator: Bryan Murray. Produced by KYUK-TV, Bethel, AK. Executive producer: Corey Flintoff. All video formats. Color. Dist.: KYUK. For additional information see KYUK VIDEO.

In 1971 the Alaska Native Claims Settlement Act (ANCSA) was passed by Congress to create legal boundaries for native-owned lands in Alaska where treaties have never been signed with the United States. Hailed at the time as a progressive solution to the recognition of land rights of Native Americans, ANCSA has in recent years been seen to pose potentially serious problems for Alaska's Indians and Inuit. In fact, the legislation may prove to be the very instrument by which they will lose their lands.

As the modern world encroached, especially following decisions to explore the Arctic for petroleum, the question of who owned the land began to be raised. In response the ANCSA was passed, creating thirteen native-owned corporations, twelve in Alaska and one in Seattle for people of Alaska native descent who live there. Forty-four million acres of public domain land and $1 billion in cash was distributed to these corporations and their constituent village corporations. Ownership of stock in the corporations was granted only to people of native descent born before 1971.

The act prohibits the sale of shares in the corporations, and exempts the land from taxes, until 1991. As that date approaches, the Alaska Federation of Natives has taken a hard look at the implications of impending stock sales and is now campaigning for changes in the act to protect the lands and to protect the corporations' stock from sales to non-natives. As the production notes, all shares are inextricably tied to the land and once that is lost the Alaska natives will have lost their most important community asset.

This investigative piece provides a clear history of the act and gives native Alaskans' perspectives on its impact. Although Congress is reviewing the legislation, the Inuit Circumpolar Conference commissioned its own study. Under the direction of noted Canadian lands claims jurist Thomas Berger, the study has now been published in book form as *Village Journey: The Report of the Alaska Native Review Commission*. By providing a timely and informative look at a situation unfamiliar to many not living in Alaska, A MATTER OF TRUST covers an important contemporary native land issue.

MAYA IN EXILE

1985, 28 min. Producers: Allan Burns and Alan Saperstein. Director: Alan Saperstein. Writer/narrator: Denise Matthews. Camera: Francois Pietri, Alan Saperstein, and Denise Matthews. ¾" vt, ½" vt (VHS, Beta). Color. In English and Spanish and Kanjobal with English voice-over. Dist.: Saperstein.

Since 1982, when the Guatemalan army stepped up its military campaign against guerrillas in the highlands, destroying Indian villages and killing at least thirty thousand people, more than one hundred thousand Maya men, women, and children have fled their country, most to Mexico. This videotape profiles an enclave of Kanjobal Maya refugees now living in Indiantown, Florida. Safe for now from bombings and massacres, the horror of their experiences is still vivid, as interviews with both adults and children show.

Scenes of their life in Indiantown show that although they have fared better than refugees in Mexico, life as exiles is not easy. They are all from the area of San Miguel Acatan and speak the Kanjobal Maya language. Despite the fact that they have formed a community together in Florida, they miss having their own land and the self-sufficiency of growing their own food. Adjusting to a cash economy, they support themselves with wage work as migrant laborers for farms in south Florida.

Although their children have learned English in school and the community is adapting to American culture, the future of the Kanjobal Maya in the United States is not assured. Under current immigration policy, some will be allowed to stay in Florida, but others are in risk of deportation, despite evidence of continuing human rights abuses in Guatemala. In presenting an informal look at the fate of a particular Maya community, this production provides a way of understanding the reasons for their flight from Guatemala and the necessity of their finding a home in the United States.

MAYA TV

1985, 10 min. Producer/directors: David Pentecost and Lyn Tiefenbacher. ¾" vt. Color. Dist.: CIMA.

Since 1980 a team of anthropological videomakers have produced videotapes filmed in highland Chiapas and the Lacandon rain forest. In MAYA TV they offer a brief yet innovative look at the techniques and symbolism of Maya weaving from the highlands. The tape also documents Sna Jolibil, a cooperative which assists weavers in mastering ancient styles and in marketing their work. It is clear that planning and cooperation play a significant role in reviving the craft of weaving and in sustaining the continuation of an artistic tradition which has been deeply intertwined with Maya identity. Designed to accompany a traveling exhibition featuring Chiapas weavings, the videotape can be screened once or looped for consecutive screenings.

A MESSAGE FROM BRAZIL

1985, 20 min. Producer/director: George C. Stoney. Assistant: Betty Puleston. Editor: Eric Early. ¾" vt, ½" vt (VHS, Beta). Color. In English, Portuguese, and Kraho. Dist.: Stoney.

Noted documentary filmmaker George Stoney has produced a videotape of a visit he made with two companions to a community of Kraho Indians living in the remote frontier area of Brazil, six hundred miles north of Brasilia in the state of Goias. In the past hundred years of contact, the Kraho have been devastated by white men's diseases and killed in frontier conflicts. Most now subsist by doing wage labor for the settlers who have taken over their lands. Harassed by poachers who kill off the game, already scarce because of the increase in settlement, the Kraho and their community are at risk. Several years ago, fifteen families decided to re-establish a traditional way of life, as a way of strengthening their culture and making a visible claim to their original lands.

In order to share their situation with Indians of North America and to affect Brazilian government policy, the Kraho participated in making this tape, which is a video "letter" from their community. It records daily life and interactions between the visitors and community members. At the heart of this production is a formal statement made by Alescho, the community leader. In it he talks of the important role of video in taking his message to the outside. Alescho's expressed wish to be able to make use of the technology is in stark contrast, poignantly felt by the viewer, to the lack of resources in his community and the difficulties for survival it faces in the immediate future. Yet Alescho's speech also suggests that in Brazil, as in other parts of Native America, access to media will increase, making possible a wide range of documentation and expression of personal and community concerns.

META MAYAN II

1981, 20 min. Producer/director/camera: Edin Velez. Producer/sound: Ethel Velez. Associate director: Eulogio Ortiz, Jr. Editor: Scott Doniger. Production assistant: Amy Rosmarin. Produced in association with the Television Lab at WNET/13, New York City. Executive producer: Carol Brandenburg. ¾" vt, ½" vt. Color. Dist.: EAI/MOMA.

Filmed in the highlands of Guatemala, META MAYAN II explores the boundary between art and documentary. Editing the tape in a repetitive, cyclical rhythm and avoiding narrative, the videomaker manipulates the images, using slow motion and frame freezing to create a "video essay." Throughout, he searches for the particular in the general view, showing an old woman laughing in a hammock, the silver drops of water flung from a piece of clothing being washed in a stream, people milling in the marketplace, and the feet of the carriers of a saint's image in a processional.

The film also provides a meditation on filming. As the camera follows a woman walking slowly down the road, she turns to look back. In the force of her gaze is seen her natural curiosity, even hostility, at being filmed. The viewer sees the complexity of the moment, of the videomaker's consciousness of his observational camera, and its possible intrusions, and of the woman's dignity and self-containment in her own world. In this moment the viewers will feel deeply that they have gained access through this videomaker's technical mastery and imagination to a world with its own meanings, symbolized through unforgettable images, which will in the end always elude the outsider's total comprehension.

Velez, well-known for his award-winning avant-garde videotapes, has also directed the documentary TULE, THE CUNA INDIANS OF SAN BLAS (for description see Volume I, p. 113–4).

MEXICO INDIGENA SERIES

Executive producers: Oscar Menendez, Juan Carlos Colín, and Juan Francisco Urrusti. For further information contact: INI or FVC-MAI.

Since 1978 the Archivo Etnografico Audiovisual of Mexico's Instituto Nacional Indigenista (INI) has undertaken a comprehensive project devoted to filming indigenous communities throughout Mexico, recording scenes of daily and ritual life and other aspects of Indian culture. Consisting of more than thirty-five documentaries, the MEXICO INDIGENA series is a remarkable achievement. The films, produced by different crews, present a thematically varied view of native Mexico today. Many works document the most traditional practices of Indian life. Others reflect the issues of culture change and economic and cultural autonomy. The films vary in style and production values; many would be improved by including a clearer discussion of the Indian communities' histories and by allowing more Indian voices to be heard.

The original 16mm films, in Spanish and indigenous languages, are available from INI. Study copies have been deposited with the Museum of the American Indian and are available for viewing at the Film and Video Center. In addition, nine of the films have been subtitled in English; some of the translations are good and others are stilted. Videotape copies of these nine are available for educational use (Dist.: FVC-MAI).

BRUJOS AND HEALERS/BRUJOS Y CURANDEROS

1981, 85 min. Producer: Miguel Camacho. Director: Juan Francisco Urrusti. Camera: Mario Luna.

The diverse uses of traditional medicine, related to magic, sorcery, and healing, are shown as practiced by mestizo, Nahua, and Zoque-Popoluca healers in the Tuxtlas region of Veracruz.

THE CRAFT OF WEAVING/EL OFICIO DE TEJER

1981, 42 min. Producer: Miguel Camacho. Director: Juan Carlos Colín. Camera: Juan Carlos Colín and Henner Hofmann.

Life in a Nahuatl-speaking Indian community in Puebla is explored. The film focuses on weaving and the problems people face in trying to subsist on the sale of their work.

HIKURI NEIRRA: LA DANZA DEL PEYOTE

1980, 32 min. Producer: Oscar Magaña. Director: Carlos Kleiman. Camera: Henner Hofmann.

This film documents Huichol ritual songs and dances during an annual celebration of the cycle of growing corn and sacred peyote.

MARA'ACAME

1982, 47 min. Producer: Raúl Alvarez. Director: Juan Francisco Urrusti. Camera: Mario Luna.

This documentary vividly portrays a Huichol *maraàcame* and aspects of his community's life in Jalisco, and focuses on his rituals of healing and religious celebration.

MITOTE TEPEHUANO

1980, 30 min. Producer: Oscar Magaña. Director: Rafael Montero. Camera: Henner Hofmann.

A ritual of the Tepehuan Indians of Durango celebrates the agricultural cycle and the initiation of the community's young people.

THE PAME/LOS PAME DE SANTA MARIA ACAPULCO

1982, 32 min. Producer: Gabriel González Souza and Mauricio Schroeder. Director: Antonio del Rivero. Camera: Arturo de la Rosa.

The ritual and cultural life of the Pame of San Luis Potosí are seen in the context of their struggle to preserve their traditions and regain their lands.

SAN PABLITO PAPER/EL PAPEL DE SAN PABLITO

1981, 33 min. Producer: Miguel Camacho. Director/camera: Federico Weingartshofer.

The Otomí community at San Pablito Pahuatlan in Puebla produces *amate* paper from tree bark. Traditionally important for healing, amate is now used to make paintings for sale to tourists and folk art collectors.

WITH THE SOUL BETWEEN THE TEETH/CON EL ALMA ENTRE LOS DIENTES

1981, 45 min. Producer: Gabriel González Souza. Director: Jaime Riestra. Camera: Pedro Torres.

Documenting traditional customs and change in a Totonac community, this film contrasts the harsh conditions facing the Indian farmers with the wealth of the mestizo ranchers living close to them.

XOCHIMILCO

1987, 90 min. Producer: Juan Francisco Urrusti. Director: Eduardo Maldonado. Camera: Santiago Navarrete.

Filmed in ancient Xochimilco, now a community of Mexico City, this documentary views a way of life which weaves together the pre-Columbian heritage with activities, both religious and secular, of today. The film includes the reflections of many Indians and mestizos on their fiestas, devotional observations, and the impact of modern urbanization.

Other titles in the series, most available for viewing at the Film and Video Center, include:

ANALCO, EL CORAZON DE UN PUEBLO *(Zapotec of Oaxaca)*

CUANDO LA NIEBLA LEVANTE *(Totonac of Puebla)*

DE BANDAS, VIDAS Y OTRES SONES *(Zapotec of Oaxaca)*

DE LA VIDA DE LOS IKOODS *(Ikoods of Oaxaca)*

DEL OTRO LADO DE LA MUERTE *(Huastec of San Luis Potosi)*

EL DIA EN QUE VINIERON LOS MUERTOS *(Mazatec of Oaxaca)*

EL ETERNO RETORNO *(Kickapoo of Coahuila and the United States)*
EN CLAVE DE SOL *(Mixe of Oaxaca)*
ENCUENTROS DE MEDICINA MAYA *(Mayas of Yucatan, Campeche, and Quintana Roo)*
FIESTA DEL SEÑOR SANTIAGO APOSTOL *(Totonac of Veracruz)*
HACH WINIK *(Lacandon of Chiapas)*
LA MUSICA Y LOS MIXES *(Mixe of Oaxaca)*
LA TIERRA DE LOS TEPEHUAS *(Tepehua of Veracruz)*
LAGUNA DE DOS TIEMPOS *(Nahua of Veracruz)*
LOA *(Totonac of Veracruz)*
MONTANA DE GUERRERO *(Nahua of Guerrero)*
ORO VERDE *(Maya of Yucatan)*
PAPALOAPAN *(Mazatec of Oaxaca)*
PELEAS DE TIGRES *(Nahua of Guerrero)*
PIOWACHUWE *(Zoque of Chiapas)*
PUREPECHAS, LOS QUE VIVEN LA VIDA *(Purepecha of Michoacan)*
QUITATE TU PA' PONERME YO *(Chinantec of Oaxaca)*
RARAMURI RA'ITSAARA *(Tarahumara of Chihuahua)*
SEMANA SANTA ENTRE LOS MAYOS *(Mayo of Sonora)*
SEMANA SANTA EN NANACATLAN *(Totonac of Puebla)*
SEMILLA DEL CUARTO SOL
UNA MAYORDOMIA *(Zoque-Popoluca of Veracruz)*

MIKEN'S WAY
For description see *Ojibway and Cree Cultural Centre Video.*

MITOTE TEPEHUANO
For description see *Mexico Indigena Series.*

MORE THAN JUST A WEEK OF FUN
For description see *Choctaw Video.*

MOUNTAIN MUSIC OF PERU
1984, 58 min. Producer/writer/camera/narrator: John Cohen. Sound: Richard Rogers. Editors: John Cohen and Jerry Michaels. In Spanish and Quechua with English subtitles and narration. 16mm, ¾" vt, ½" vt. Color. Dist.: Cinema Guild.

The musical thread which runs through the Andes extends back thousands of years. Although adapting instruments introduced by the Spanish, it has retained much of its characteristic flavor. This documentary moves from small towns and remote mountain villages to the capital city of Lima, examining the reflection of native and mestizo culture in music. Cohen shows the richness of indigenous music and defends the Indians' right to greater social power. He is concerned that the seven million Indians in Peru, who form the majority of the population, continue to be seen by the cultural elite as a minority.

Musical performance of various kinds is filmed at different locations. At Q'eros, remotely situated at fourteen thousand feet in the Andes, traditional Quechua songs and flute music for a ritual are performed. In Lima a social club of immigrants from Ayacucho meets on weekends to dance the traditional scissors dance to music typical of their region. Miners assembled in the capital at a political encampment are shown protesting their situation in songs. Today's popular music in Peru, played on radio and records, is a synthesis based on indigenous music.

However, in urban Peru much native music and culture is ignored. Near Cuzco the touristic performance of Inti Rayma, advertised as the annual Inca festival of the sun, celebrates only Indians of the past, ignoring their contemporary presence in the society. In the northern Andean town of Huaylas the annual fiesta is filled with music and dance but, despite the fact that most people have an Indian heritage, indigenous culture is not celebrated. However, throughout the film, Cohen assembles a selection of music performances whose overall message is that an Indian heritage is at the core of Peruvian cultural life and, though not always acknowledged, it will endure in both its traditional forms and new popular music styles.

Cohen has documented Andean culture and arts in other films, including A CONTINUOUS WARP and Q'EROS: THE SHAPE OF SURVIVAL (for descriptions see Volume I, p. 34 and p. 97). In CHOQELA: ONLY INTERPRE-TATION, concerned with a traditional oral song cycle, he contrasts its interpretation by the native community with that of outsiders. (Dist.: Cinema Guild).

MUSIC AND DANCE OF THE MOHAWK

1983, 25 min. Producer/director/camera/editor: Frank Semmens. Executive producer: Akwesasne Museum. 16mm, ¾" vt. Dist.: Image.

"The people must have a song . . . it's one of the oldest laws, from when the world was first made," says traditional Mohawk chief Tom Porter, addressing a crowd gathered for a traditional celebration at the St. Regis-Akwesasne (Mohawk) Reservation on the New York-Canadian border. The spiritual significance of music and dance for traditional Mohawks is the subject of this videotape. The production also documents the making of musical instruments, as craftsman Harold Thomas demonstrates how he makes a water drum and a horn rattle.

Francis Boots and Ron LaFrance discuss how the forms of various dances reflect a philosophy which values humanity's respect for the earth and its creatures. The round dance, for example, is both a celebration and a symbolic reminder that man is but one element in a whole cycle of creation. Other dances may be dedicated to a specific creature, such as the Rabbit Dance, based on an ancient story, that continues to honor the rabbit as man's fellow species.

LaFrance explains that dance is also an important part of the continuation of Mohawk culture because it reflects events in history. For example, the Moccasin Dance, a "new" dance from about 1800, originated during the years of Iroquois involvement in the fur trade. He affirms that to keep Mohawk culture alive it is necessary to continue to dance and to teach the meanings behind the songs and dances to the young.

An earlier production by Semmens which documents an important traditional art is MOHAWK BASKETMAKING (see description in Volume I, p. 79).

NOMADS OF THE RAIN FOREST

1984, 59 min. Producer/writer: Grant G. Behrman. Director: Adrian Warren. Associate producer/writer: Robert E. Dierbeck. Camera: Hugh Maynard. Sound: Joel Rettig. Editor: Peter Scheer. Music: Ted Moore. Anthropological consultant/writer: James A. Yost. Produced by WGBH-TV, Boston, for the series NOVA. ¾" vt, ½" vt. Color. Dist.: UCEMC.

The Waorani Indians, who inhabit the rain forest at the headwaters of the Amazon in eastern Ecuador, have lived in isolation from other tribes for hundreds of years. Their traditional lands covered approximately eight thousand square miles of the forest, where they remained largely undisturbed because of their hostility toward outsiders. Today only a few families remain, hunting game with blowguns and spears and cultivating gardens. Most of the tribe has been settled on a government protectorate.

NOMADS OF THE RAIN FOREST was produced during a 1983 multidisciplinary expedition to research the Waorani. It briefly introduces the team involved with making this film, including Grant Behrman of The Explorer's Club, anthropologist James Yost who is an authority on Waorani language and culture, and noted Amazonian scholar Robert Carneiro.

This ethnographic documentary is concerned with a community of four families still living in the forest. Family life is seen as harmonious and cooperative. Although men and women do different work, they are viewed as equals and there seems to be no experience of competition. Children have nearly the same status as adults, and watch and learn from them. Sequences document traditional technologies and Waorani values. Scenes of family life, activities of the young, and horticulture are included.

Hunting skills are well portrayed, from the making of curare and blowguns to several scenes of hunting. Two small boys cooperate easily as they hunt together with one blowgun. In one of the best sequences of Indian hunting on film, which opens and concludes the film, 60-year-old Campeti and his young assistant pursue a howler monkey through the forest, climbing towering trees and running along the forest floor after it. It is grueling work heightened by the direct camera work and recording of natural sound. The narration provides additional insight by noting that today the success of a hunt is more difficult to attain, since the rain forest is rapidly being destroyed.

The aggressiveness to outsiders for which this tribe has been known is referred to early in the film through the inclusion of footage shot in the 1950's by missionaries who were killed by the Indians within minutes of the filming. This view of the Waorani contrasts with what is seen in the rest of the film, which explores the cooperative relationships and skills of their remarkably egalitarian society.

NORTH AMERICAN INDIANS AND EDWARD S. CURTIS

1985, 28 min. Producer/director: Teri C. McLuhan. Camera: Robert Fiore. Editor: Charlotte Zwerin. 16mm, ¾" vt. Color. Dist.: Phoenix/BFA.

This film focuses on Edward S. Curtis (1868–1952), whose life work was concerned with preserving a record of North American Indians and Alaskan Eskimos. It is edited from THE SHADOW CATCHER, an 88-minute film produced by McLuhan in 1974 (see description in Volume I, p. 102–3). The shorter version permits more audiences, particularly schools and educational television, to become familiar with the life and accomplishments of this controversial and fascinating photographer, filmmaker, and writer.

This shortened film is a different documentary altogether from THE SHADOW CATCHER. One of the great strengths of the original film was its interviews with Indian people — Navajo, Pueblo, Kwakiutl — on the impact of photography and film. These are omitted from this version. Thus the Indian "voice," so successfully juxtaposed to Curtis' own strong vision in the earlier film, is missing. The shortened film is, however, a very good portrait of the American photographer most famous for producing romantic images of Indians, with their breathtaking beauty and sometimes unrealistic nostalgia.

NORTHWEST ARCTIC VIDEO

Northwest Arctic Television Center Director: Bob Walker. All programs available on ¾" vt, ½" vt. (1" vt by special request). Color. In Inupiaq or English. Dist.: Northwest Arctic.

The Northwest Arctic Television Center was opened at Kotzebue, Alaska, in 1979, funded by Alaska's Department of Education. The primary purpose of the Center is to produce programs about cultural, social, and political issues pertinent to the region, including documentaries of traditional skills, public affairs programs, and looks at specific aspects of cultural transition in Inupiat Eskimo culture. Student video from the region, programs for in-service training in skills needed by teachers, and programs on Inuit studies are also available. Two productions are described under their individual titles:

SHUNGNAK: A VILLAGE PROFILE
INUPIAT ESKIMO HEALING

For a complete listing contact the distributor. Some other productions include the following:

THE ALASKA NATIVE CLAIMS SETTLEMENT ACT SERIES

16–30 min. each.

In five educational programs, with student reader and teacher's guide available, the terms and implications of this major legislation are explored, through an examination of its history, how it has settled native land claims and established native corporations, and what its impact may be in the future.

INUPIAT LEGENDS OF THE NORTHWEST ARCTIC SERIES

18–25 minutes each. In Inupiaq with English subtitles.

Elders of the region tell stories passed down through many generations, including the tales of Raven and Mink's Feast and the Twins of Kiana. Production of this series is on-going; contact the distributor for a complete list of stories.

TRADITIONAL INUPIAT ESKIMO HEALTH SERIES

These programs, developed to preserve traditional Inupiat healing techniques, are used in training health practitioners throughout Northwest Alaska. Native doctors show how to treat a variety of illnesses, from arthritis and skin problems to dislocations and backaches. Each was recorded on location and some are produced with bilingual narration, one channel in Inupiaq and the other English.

Community Health Aides: The Vital Link *(29 min.)*
Ignipkainailhat/Traditional Prenatal Care *(Parts I & II, 30 min. each)*
Ilussig and Uniqtit/Manipulation and Dislocation *(22 min.)*

64

Iyat/Hot Springs *(14 min.)*
Kapi/Poking and Bloodletting *(16 min.)*

TRADITIONAL INUPIAT ESKIMO TECHNOLOGY SERIES

These videotapes document subsistence skills and methods for making implements and kayaks. The programs show elders on location at their homes and seasonal camps who demonstrate their techniques:

Auvirinmi/At Summer Sealing Camp *(23 min.)*
How They Did the Caribou *(19 min.)*
Making a Beaver Hat *(12 min.)*
Making a Birchbark Basket *(12 min.)*
Making a Harpoon *(27 min.)*
Making a Qayaq *(Part I-7 min., Part II-15 min.)*
Making an Ulu (Woman's Knife) *(19 min.)*
Making and Filling a Seal Puuq (Bag) *(15 min.)*
Putting Away Ugruk (Bearded Seal) Flippers *(5 min.)*
Sheefish Gill Netting *(5 min.)*
Ice Fishing For Sheefish *(13 min.)*
Snaring Rabbits *(13 min.)*

OJIBWAY AND CREE CULTURAL CENTRE VIDEO

Executive producer: Dennis Austin. ¾" vt, ½" vt. Color. Dist.: Ojibway and Cree.

Since 1979 the Ojibway and Cree Cultural Centre in Timmins, Ontario, has produced over twenty-five videotapes which portray traditional craft techniques, tales, and profiles of elders. The programs, which have local communities as their target audience, reflect the heritage of Indians in eastern Canada. Made with simple means, the productions demonstrate that video can be an invaluable tool for preserving aspects of community life and native traditions. For a complete list of titles contact the distributor.

A selection includes:

THE BUSH TOBOGGAN *(1984, 20 min.)*

John Paul Spence demonstrates and explains the traditional method of making a toboggan from the wood of the ash tree. Because the toboggan can be made with only a few lightweight tools and materials available in the bush, it has traditionally been made by hunters and travelers in need of transporting their catch or goods when far from home.

DAVID CHARLES *(1986, 22 min.)*

Seated before a birchbark wigwam and dressed in traditional clothing, elder David Charles speaks in his language to Ojibway and Cree young people and demonstrates various traditional skills, including drumming and singing, the making of a bow and snowshoes, and cooking meat in a box with hot rocks. The tape concludes with a powwow held in his honor.

THE DRUM *(1982, 30 min.)*

A gathering on the St. Regis-Akwesasne (Mohawk) Reservation is filmed, at which traditional chief Tom Porter and other participants discuss the drum as sacred and the role music plays in the life of the people.

MIKEN'S WAY *(1985, 15 min.)*

Miken Patrick is the subject of a memorial portrait in which people comment on him as a gifted teacher of traditional skills, remembering him for his patience, generosity, and humor.

STICKS AND STONES, LEATHER AND BONES *(1986, 30 min.)*

Hosts Norman Wesley and Mary Lou Iahtail demonstrate various games and amusements they played when young, including bone and sinew roarers, "to string them" (a game of focus and dexterity), string figures, and making a "pop gun" using moss pellets.

THE TRADITIONAL SNOWSHOE *(1984, 27 min.)*

John Paul Spence shows steps in making snowshoes, including locating materials, carving and bending the frame, and weaving the webbing.

OLD DANCES, NEW DANCERS

For description see *KYUK Video.*

ONENHAKENRA: WHITE SEED

1984, 20 min. Producer/director/camera: Frank Semmens. Produced by the Akwesasne Museum. Executive producer: Salli M. Benedict. 16mm, ¾" vt, ½" vt. Color. For distribution information contact: Akwesasne Museum.

The Akwesasne Museum on the St. Regis-Akwesasne Reservation has produced films, videotapes, and slide productions concerned with Mohawk culture. ONENHAKENRA explores the use and significance of corn as a traditional food, tracing its meaning to its origins as a sacred gift from Sky Woman. As a growing plant, it involves the work of men and women, boys and girls. Corn is called Grandmother, reflecting the Iroquois belief that women are the center of the family. As a durable staple and a food developed by Native Americans, corn functions as a symbol of Indian self-sufficiency.

Preparation of corn for storage and ways to cook corn dishes, such as traditional corn soup, are shown. One woman speaks of her frequent craving for Mohawk corn bread, and demonstrates how it is prepared. Corn husk dolls, no longer just for children, are made, treasured now as a traditional Mohawk art form. The film focuses on corn and people's reflections on its use as a way of presenting the audience with a view of Mohawk traditions. ONENHAKENRA conveys even sacred beliefs without showing ceremonies on film, and has succeeded in documenting a community which has often perceived filmmaking as an unwelcome intrusion.

OUR CHILDREN ARE OUR FUTURE

1981, 57 min. Producer/director: Tony Snowsill. Associate producer/editor: Christine Welsh. Camera: Mark Irwin and Bob Nichol. Sound: Ian Hendry and Martin Fossum. 16mm, ¾" vt, ½" vt (VHS, Beta). Dist.: Direction (US)/CLC (Canada)

In both Canada and the United States intense pressures face native families, including lack of economic opportunity, housing shortages, loss of culture, and high rates of alcoholism and suicide. As a growing number of Indian people leave the economic and social problems they face on their reserves and reservations for a life in the city, family problems can intensify. OUR CHILDREN

ARE OUR FUTURE focuses on the policies of the Canadian child welfare system (which are similar to those of the United States) and suggests that alternatives exist which can avoid some of the system's worst problems.

Filmed in the western cities of Edmonton, Regina, and Vancouver and at the Blackfoot Indian Reserve in Alberta, this film investigates the needs of Indian children placed into foster care. A family court worker who is Indian and two mothers describe the cycle of poverty faced by Indian families who have moved to cities and the pain of losing their children as a result.

OUR CHILDREN ARE OUR FUTURE follows the lives of two children, one placed in a non-native foster home, and the other in an on-reserve foster home. The problem of alienation caused by removing Indian children from native environments and its destructive effect on young lives is illustrated in the case of Michael, a 20-year-old Cree Indian from Fort Chipewyan in northern Saskatchewan, now serving a term in prison for armed robbery. Both he and his non-Indian foster parents relate their perceptions of what happened to Michael and why. The film also tells the story of Chip, who was placed with an Indian foster family on the Blackfoot Reserve, from which his family had moved to the city after he was born. His success shows that Indian foster children may not face the same degree of difficulty if reared in an Indian environment.

The problem of Indian child welfare is not a new one and the statistics are alarming. In Saskatchewan, for example, sixty percent of the children being cared for by child welfare services are Indian. The film presents convincing evidence that there will be much human suffering and loss of potential for these young people. This film shows the magnitude of the pressures on Indian people, and the frustrating certainty that current policies, in both Canada and the United States, are not providing adequately for Indian needs.

OUR LIVES IN OUR HANDS

1986, 44 min. Producers: Karen Carter and Harald Prins. Director: Karen Carter. Camera: Eric Muzzy and Robert Brady. Sound: Stuart Mann. Editor: Bruce Jehle. Music: Stuart Diamond. Sponsored by the Aroostook Micmac Council. 16mm, ¾" vt, ½" vt. Color. Dist.: DER.

OUR LIVES IN OUR HANDS presents the story of the Micmac basketmakers of Aroostook County, Maine, focusing on a man of quiet strength, Donald Sanipass, and members of his extended family. As Maine's northernmost county, this is an area where prospects for employment are grim. Micmac baskets have long been used by the "stoop workers," both Indian and non-Indian, who harvest the potato fields. With the increasing mechanization of potato farming, the demand for potato baskets has declined dramatically. Micmacs speak of their experience doing wage labor during the harvest and discuss how their livelihood as basketmakers has relied on this industry.

As the basketmakers are shown selecting and felling an ash tree, pounding logs into splints, shaving splints, and weaving the baskets, they talk about the role this craft has played in their families and their hopes that the young generation will learn these skills. Baskets are sold to middlemen for resale. However, the local market is so depressed that, to encourage the continuation of the craft, the Aroostook Micmac Council has started a marketing cooperative run by tribe members called "The Basket Bank."

Along with the survival of basketmaking, the survival of their language and the hope to obtain a tribal land base are issues of concern today. In fact, the Aroostook Micmac Council was initially organized to assist the Micmacs in their struggle for recognition of federal tribal status and their aboriginal land rights, such as other Maine tribes received in 1980. The filmmakers worked closely with the Council to provide a view of the Micmac consistent with the way they view themselves.

OUR SACRED LAND

1984, 28 min. Producer/director: Chris Spotted Eagle. Camera: Michael Chin and Ed Matrey. Sound: John Penny. Editor: Greg Cummins. Original music: Kevin Clarke. Narrator: Chris Cavendar. Produced for the Corporation for Public Broadcasting. 16mm, ¾" vt, ½" vt (VHS, Beta). Color. Dist.: Spotted Eagle/Intermedia.

OUR SACRED LAND, by Native American independent filmmaker Chris Spotted Eagle, provides a view of an important contemporary issue and shows how strongly sacred places and practices continue to be valued by native people. The film focuses on the story of the continuing struggle of the Sioux to regain the Black Hills of South Dakota. Although guaranteed to them in 1868 by the Treaty of Fort Laramie, their lands were later taken by an act of Congress and opened up to mining and settlement.

The film examines the reasons why many Sioux have refused to accept the $105 million recently awarded by the American government for the lands' confiscation, despite the fact that the tribe is impoverished. Embedded in this conflict is the issue of Indian religious freedom and the difficulties posed them in pursuing their beliefs and sacred practices. For traditional Sioux the Black Hills are the center of spiritual life, and sites like Harney Peak and Bear Butte are religious shrines. As federal lands, however, these mountains are also commercial recreation centers, used by hikers and campers, who sometimes disturb Indian people who pray and fast at these sacred sites.

Speakers in the film include elders such as Matthew King, Sioux lawyers and tribal leaders, and participants in the Yellow Thunder encampment which has tried to re-establish a Sioux way of life close to the land and sacred sites. Their commitment to the struggle is well-expressed in the words of Tony Fast Horse, now Chief Judge for the Oglala Sioux Tribal Court at Pine Ridge Reservation. "(My ancestors) travelled to Washington with this treaty in their hands . . . Now I am carrying the document in my hands. If I am unsuccessful, one of my children is going to inherit this document . . . Someday some great-grandchild of mine is going to say, 'My grandfather was steadfast in his right to the Black Hills.'"

Spotted Eagle has made other productions on Native Americans and the issues of religious freedom, cultural survival, and education, including CELEBRATION, THE GREAT SPIRIT WITHIN THE HOLE, and HEART OF THE EARTH SURVIVAL SCHOOL (see descriptions in this volume).

OUR SONGS WILL NEVER DIE

For description see *Shenandoah Films.*

THE PAME/LOS PAME DE SANTA MARIA ACAPULCO

For description see *Mexico Indigena Series.*

68

THE PANARE: SCENES FROM THE FRONTIER

1983, 55 min. Director: Chris Curling. Camera: Maurice Fisher. Sound: Roger Long. Editor: Ian Pitch. Consultant anthropologist: Paul Henley. Produced for the BBC-TV series Worlds Apart. *Series producers: Chris Curling and Melissa Llewellyn-Davies. 16mm, ¾" vt. Color. Dist.: FI.*

In Venezuela today, two thousand Panare Indians continue much of their traditional way of life, still depending for their survival on the game and fish they hunt daily. For generations these Indians have peacefully co-existed with the Spanish-speaking cattle herders who share their land. Until now the settlers in their region have been grazing their animals without destroying the forests and rivers in which the Panare hunt and fish. Slowly this situation is changing.

The film documents the Panare as they pursue their annual hunt in the highlands to get food for an important feast and ritual to be held later in the season. It shows their techniques for hunting the various species, with blowguns and shot guns, and of preparing the food for eating. It also focuses on the changes in their indigenous area that have already begun to affect their lives.

As a group of Panare walk across the plain towards their hunting grounds, they carry with them prized equipment, including bicycles, which have come with the increased settlement of non-Indians in the area. As they pass, settlers comment on the Indians, demonstrating their lack of knowledge about them. The two groups, however, will together face development; the simple paths they both use for travel soon will be replaced by highways. In interviews several of the Panare discuss their expectations for the future.

The Indians' lands are a frontier where settlement and large-scale development projects are planned. A huge bauxite mine, which will inevitably have a devastating effect on the ecology, is soon to be built in the area. The film poses the question of whether the Panare can survive the expansion of development. They have no treaties guaranteeing legal title to the traditional hunting and fishing grounds which we see them utilize in the film. They, and countless tribes of the Amazonian rain forest, face an uncertain future.

PARLEZ-VOUS YUP'IK?
For description see *KYUK Video.*

THE PATH OF OUR ELDERS
For description see *Shenandoah Films.*

PEOPLE OF KASHUNUK
For description see *KYUK Video.*

THE PIPE IS THE ALTAR
For description see *Celebration.*

POETAS CAMPESINOS
For description see *Maria Sabina.*

POPOL VUH: THE CREATION MYTH OF THE MAYA

1986, 29 min. Producer/director/animator: Patricia Amlin. Narrator: Luis Valdez. Characters'
voices: El Teatro Campesino. Music: Todd Boekelheide. Color. 16mm, ¾" vt, ½" vt.
Dist.: UCEMC.

This beautifully animated film portrays the first part of the great religious epic
of the Maya of southern Mexico and Central America, using an ancient version
first written in Quiché Maya in the sixteenth century. POPOL VUH brings
to life many mythological themes, convincingly evoking the process of metamor-
phosis and transformation central to the Maya story. It tells of the creation of
the world, the birth and death of the First Fathers in the Underworld, the defeat
of the Evil Ones by the Sacred Mother, and the birth of the Hero Twins.

Unlike many animated films of the traditional tales, POPOL VUH sparkles
with visual energy and a sense of deep involvement with the epic it portrays.
Its imagery is drawn directly from paintings on Maya funerary ceramics over
a thousand years old, and its musical score is played on authentic pre-Columbian
instruments. The film will appeal to audiences of all ages, as it vividly presents
a tale which is by turns humorous, adventurous, frightening, and profound.
Teachers' guides for elementary and secondary instruction are available from
the distributor.

PRIDE, PURPOSE, PROMISE: PAIUTES OF THE SOUTHWEST

1984, 30 min. Producer/writer: Mitchell Fox. Camera/editor: Julie A. Smith. Produced by KLVX-
TV, Las Vegas. ¾" vt. Color. Dist.: NAPBC.

Concerned with tribal self-determination, this production presents the history
and the current situation of several Southern Paiute communities in Arizona,
Utah, and Nevada. It demonstrates how significant tribal status can be for both
economic self-sufficiency and improvement of the quality of life in Indian communities. The communities are small, with different needs. For the Utah Paiutes
the recent restoration of tribal status now offers a better chance to reduce their
enormous poverty. Although more prosperous, the Kaibab Paiutes of northern
Arizona have found it difficult to establish Indian enterprises. Their tribal
chairman, Bill Tom, speaks of his hopes for developing both agriculture and
tourism.

In southeastern Nevada the Paiute community had been torn apart by
many conflicts until the establishment of their Moapa Reservation. The tribe,
working with federal agencies under the Indian Self-Determination and Educational Assistance Act, has inaugurated its own enterprise, greenhouse agriculture. The Las Vegas Paiute live in the middle of a very neglected metropolitan
area. As a tax-exempt group, the tribe makes its income from tax-free sales to
Indians and non-Indians. However, the constant contact with urban life and
television culture causes many to worry about their young people's future.

This local public affairs television production, with interviews and voice-
over narrative dominating, provides a view of several tribes of similar background
in the same region, who nevertheless live in remarkably different circumstances.
It also explores the impact on native tribes of various federal policies. As the
only production on contemporary Southern Paiute communities, it is a welcome
addition to the works now available on Native American life today.

THE PROBABLE PASSING OF ELK CREEK

1982, 60 min. Producer/director/writer/narrator: Rob Wilson. Camera: Mahlon Picht and William Zarchy. Produced for KTEH-TV, San Jose, CA. 16mm, ¾" vt, ¾" vt. Color. Dist.: Cinema Guild.

This film, about events in a rural valley in northern California, looks at the passing of a small town's way of life and presents a view of a nearby Indian community living in isolation from its white neighbors. It illustrates a dilemma common to many reservations. The people are being asked to choose between economic improvement through the sale of resources and the enhancement of tradition and cultural continuity which depends on their retaining their lands.

The state of California has announced plans to build a reservoir which would displace people from the town of Elk Creek and completely cover the Grindstone Creek Indian Reservation. The decision to proceed with its construction lies in the Indian community's hands. Although a hundred years earlier they were forced by settlers to move to another site, they hold title to their present and former lands in the valley and have the power to force out the descendants of the settlers who live there.

The neighboring Indian and white communities both call the valley home but do not seem to share it, apparently living in separate worlds. Each community is grounded in vastly different histories and sense of belonging there, a situation typical in many places in the United States. Perhaps unintentionally, the structure of the film reinforces this lack of shared place or community by presenting each group of people in their own mini-documentary within the program, and by focusing mainly on the white town.

The Indian leaders are concerned about the choice they must make. Although the dam would produce income from the sale of land, it would also flood the lands they consider home. They speak of their current efforts to preserve tribal values, such as having recently constructed a dance lodge in the traditional architectural style. The program concludes with the decision still being weighed. Told from the point of view of a young reporter, the production is as much a record of his responses to the situation in the valley as it is of the communities there.

RETURN TO SOVEREIGNTY: SELF DETERMINATION AND THE KANSAS KICKAPOO

1982, 46 min. Producer/writer: Donald D. Stull. Director/writer/editor: David M. Kendall. Writer/narrator: Bernard Hirsch. Camera: Ward H. Bryant. ¾" vt, ½" vt. Color. Dist.: UCEMC.

In 1975 the Indian Self-Determination and Educational Assistance Act (ISDEAA) was passed in recognition that Native American communities have been overly dominated by the federal government. The law seeks to "provide maximum Indian participation in the government and education of the Indian people." RETURN TO SOVEREIGNTY examines how this legislation is being implemented among the Kansas Kickapoo.

Through interviews with tribal administrators and elders, the local superintendent for the Bureau of Indian Affairs, and specialists in Indian law and history, the production documents how this tribe has tried to reclaim its sovereign powers. But the Kickapoo are still struggling, as the audience learns when tribal members speak of their hopes and frustrations.

Noting the major funding provisions of the ISDEAA, the film traces the flow of monies into the Kickapoo tribal government for construction of numerous buildings, including a library and a senior citizen's center, for instituting a tribal business, and for its schools. However, no funds were made available for books for the empty library or for an initial outlay for merchandise to sell in the new tribal store. Under the guise of "sovereignty" the Kickapoos have gained some control over tribal programs, but without a means for economic independence, they continue to need support from the government.

It is nearly impossible to attract private industry to the reservation. The new enterprise, a tribally controlled agricultural project, is active, but it is not competitive with surrounding farms which have been in operation for many generations. In only one area has the tribe met with real success in determining the structure and function of its own institutions. The Kansas Kickapoo have established their own school system, close to the community and with a largely Kickapoo faculty. Federal financial assistance has been crucial in inaugurating the necessary changes.

This production, somewhat choppy in style, covers a number of issues, and relies heavily on interviews. As an exploration of current federal Indian policy, it is extremely valuable. The case of the Kansas Kickapoo demonstrates that government assistance continues to remain necessary for many Native American tribes to firmly establish a base for their autonomy and self-sufficiency.

Other films by producer Donald Stull on the history and culture of Indians in Kansas include NESHNABEK (see Volume I, p. 87) and ANOTHER WIND IS MOVING, concerned with the boarding school experience (both distributed by UCEMC).

REVIVAL
1983, 29 min. Producer/directors: Michael Brodie and Bill Roxborough. Narrator: Doreen Jensen. ¾" vt, ½" vt. (VHS, Beta). Color. Dist.: Matrix/VOI.

The four contemporary artists featured in this production work in the Northwest Coast artistic tradition, which in recent decades has found expression in both in traditional forms and new ones, such as silkscreen prints and jewelry. Much of their art is made to be used, as seen in the eagle headpiece by Haida artist Reg Davidson and the button blanket by Dorothy Grant, also Haida. Nishga artist Norman Tait oversees the printing of a silkscreened design of the beaver, his clan crest. In addition to being sold to collectors, these prints will be given away as gifts in a potlatch ceremony.

These artists look to the artists of old to interpret the design vocabulary of the Northwest Coast tradition. The production includes an animation which describes the basic shapes and combinations of design elements typical of the region's styles. Noreen Jensen, Gitskan carver, demonstrates the use of a pattern and template for making a mask. Each of the artists discusses the personal and cultural significance of the objects they make, and how the practice of their art is a vital means of participating in their culture heritage. Producers Brodie and Roxborough have also documented artists participating in a 1983 Canadian conference in NATIONAL NATIVE ARTISTS SYMPOSIUM (Dist.: VOI) and noted artist ROBERT DAVIDSON (see below).

ROBERT DAVIDSON

1981, 29 min. Producer/directors: Michael Brodie and Bill Roxborough. ¾" vt, ½" vt (VHS, Beta). Color. In English or French. Dist.: Matrix/VOI.

Produced for Native American studies programs in British Columbia, this excellent work on Northwest Coast art features one of the best-known of contemporary Indian artists, Robert Davidson. He is shown making a deer skin drum, with the entire process well portrayed, beginning with the preparation of the hide and concluding with a depiction of how Davidson determines the design and its shape for the drum. The artist is impassioned and articulate as he discusses his techniques, the philosophy behind the art of the Haida, and his personal connection to it.

Steeped in Haida tradition, Davidson sees art as but one strand in a web of cultural connections. Part of his own sense of his ability to make this drum is his understanding of the role of the Haida language and knowledge of the songs and ceremonies for which it is intended. Davidson feels a responsibility to help perpetuate Haida traditions, illustrated as he gently interacts with his child in the studio. He says "Sometimes I can't find the strength to carry what has been given to me, but I have to find the strength to demonstrate my knowledge and understanding to the children." In fact, the drum he is making will be given away at a potlatch to encourage young people to learn the songs.

The production ends with Davidson and other men, filmed at his family's fishing camp near Masset in the Queen Charlotte Islands, sharing songs on the now-completed drum. A study guide is available from the distributors.

ROCK ART TREASURES OF ANCIENT AMERICA: THE CALIFORNIA COLLECTION

1983, 25 min. Producer/director: Dave Caldwell. Writer: David S. Whitley. Camera: Duane Anderly, Kevin McNally, and Steve Shapiro. Editor: Bruce Motyer. Narrator: Scott Beach. 16mm, ¾" vt, ½" vt (VHS, Beta). Color. Dist.: Caldwell.

The appreciation and conservation of the complex and enigmatic rock art of ancient Native Americans has been established as a priority by scholars in the field. ROCK ART TREASURES focuses on three major types of rock art — carvings, paintings, and ground figures — at three sites in southern California with spectacular examples of the work. Inset into the film are contemporary Indian storytellers from tribes near these sites, telling traditional tales complementary to the imagery of the ancient art. The film stresses that early native groups used it to seek ways of influencing hostile environments or to explain the workings of the cosmos.

Beautiful footage has been shot of the Shoshone petroglyphs at the National Historical Landmark at China Lake, the Mojave intaglios along the southern end of the Colorado River, and the Chumash cave paintings at Los Padres National Forest. Native stories include a Shoshone Coyote tale told by Dugan Hansen, and a Chumash tale about the primacy of the sun, by Victor "Sky Eagle" Lopez. A tale of the culture hero Mostampo by Tarahumara storyteller Helen Johangsten is a rich narrative, but its inclusion suggests inaccurately a direct relationship between this tribe and the geoglyphs of the southern Colorado River.

The film presents a generalized view of Native American prehistory and mythic thought, and touches on specifics by presenting the tales. It employs a score of electronic music and many photographic devices, including a large number of helicopter shots and the use of distorting lenses and superimpositions, but sometimes seems overly contrived. Although technically more complicated than seems necessary, the film is of great value in offering an examination of these impressive Native American sites.

ROPE TO OUR ROOTS

1981, 30 min. Producer/director/writer: Bo Boudart. Associate producer/sound: Elizabeth O'Connell. Produced for the Inuit Life Foundation. 16mm, ¾" vt, ½" vt. Color. Dist.: Boudart.

This film of the Inuit Circumpolar Conference (ICC), an international organization of Eskimos and Inuit from Alaska, Canada, and Greenland founded in 1977, was made during their second meetings, held in Greenland in June 1980. Commonalities and differences in life styles and concerns lead to a lively exchange of views among the delegates. Issues discussed include health care, communication between peoples of the Arctic, education, and development policies for the circumpolar region.

All share concerns about the threat of losing their lands and aboriginal rights, especially in the face of recent exploration for oil and other resources. In Canada and Greenland no treaties or legislation exist to guarantee the Inuit their lands, as eloquently described by the first Inuit member of the Canadian parliament. In the United States plans for the Alaskan oil pipeline forced the federal government to make a legal settlement in 1971, but the law was passed without input from native people and poses problems for the continued survival of their village communities.

Scenes of traditional whale hunting are juxtaposed with those of a supertanker in the Beaufort Sea which will follow shipping lanes passing through whale and walrus breeding areas. Two elders speak of the great damage wrought by even a small oil spill, and the specter of a gigantic spill is raised. By the conference's end, the ICC has formed resolutions for protecting the marine habitat from offshore drilling and other resource development.

Although primarily a record of a conference, ROPE TO OUR ROOTS is so well edited that it provides a consistently interesting survey of the concerns of Arctic peoples. The film succeeds in demonstrating the necessity for more political action in the Arctic. It also shows able leaders articulating local and regional concerns and uniting in a unique international native organization to press for solutions to common problems.

SACRED CIRCLE *and* SACRED CIRCLE—RECOVERY

1980, 29 min. each. Producer/director: Donald K. Spence. Writers: Donald K. Spence and Earle Waugh. Camera: Doug Cole. Narrator: Adrian Hope. Music: Robert Durkach. Produced by the Department of Religious Studies, University of Alberta. 16mm, ¾" vt. Color. Dist.: UAL.

SACRED CIRCLE

The spiritual world view of the Plains Indians is presented in this production, which combines an imaginative use of music with excellent cinematography. The narrator, a Cree-Métis elder, explains man's relationship to the earth and animal life, and introduces the roles of the sacred pipe, sweetgrass, and the vision quest.

As a focus of Plains Indian ceremonial life, the Sun Dance is discussed in detail. Historical photographs, representing several different tribes, are linked together to create a feeling of the deep significance of this ritual. Not only is the description informative, it also conveys a sense of the immediacy and the holiness of the event. Although showing a contemporary Sun Dance lodge, the production neglects to mention that the Sun Dance, once banned by white authorities, is a vital and growing observance on the Plains today.

SACRED CIRCLE — RECOVERY

A second film examines contemporary native spirituality and religion in Canada. It traces the history of the transformation of Indian belief systems with the arrival of the Europeans. In interviews people speak of the damage done to them by the missionary and boarding school experiences, tracing cultural disintegration and personal experiences with alcohol and drug abuse to the loss of their own spiritual ways.

Some traditions, however, have survived intact and other have been adapted by Indian people to a Christian context. Both types of contemporary spiritual practice are shown, in a traditional ceremony held by members of the Dené Thá Band and a Catholic pilgrimage to a sacred lake. The focus of this production is on the benefit to young Native Americans of rediscovering their spirituality through native practices like the sweat lodge and vision quest.

SALMON ON THE RUN

1980–81, 58 min. Producer/director/camera/editor: Steve Christiansen. Producer/director/writer: Jim Mayer. Producer/sound: Lynn Adler. Produced by WGBH-TV, Boston, for the series NOVA. ¾" vt, ½" vt (VHS, Beta). Color. Dist.: TLV.

An independent production company went to the Klamath River area of northern California and Oregon to produce a documentary on salmon and to focus on conditions threatening the survival of the salmon species of the Northwest Coast. The program opens with interviews presenting the interests, sometimes conflicting, of the Indian, sports, commercial, and industrial salmon fisherman.

In investigating the problem of the overall decline of the salmon population, it explores how salmon and the people who depend on them for livelihood have been affected by industrialization, as well as by the marketing of water and electrical power. In this analysis the ecological changes brought about by lumbering, ocean fish farming, and agribusiness (frequently operated by the same companies) are shown to be the major reason for the salmon's decline.

For the Yurok Indians of California, salmon fishing is an ancient tradition. In the 1970's Indian protests in this region led to the federal hearings which confirmed that the Yurok and other tribes have been guaranteed by treaty the right to fish in the river exempt from the state regulations which govern other fishermen. Their fishing rights have brought them into conflict with sports fishermen and small-scale commercial fishermen who strongly resent what they feel is special access to the salmon permitted Indians, who are allowed to fish with nets in addition to rod and reel.

This production shows a far more complex picture, in which Indians, even those whose catch will be marketed, barely affect the salmon population, which struggles to survive the sophisticated techniques of industrial fisheries and the pollution and damming of streams by lumber and power industries. Focused at its center on the survival of salmon species, the production presents ever-widening circles of cause-and-effect, showing that a natural ecology is intrinsic to the survival of species. Industry's lack of interest in preserving the ecology stems from the expanding needs of consumers who live far from this region. For example, as species die out from their native rivers, industrial fishing replaces them with species less genetically varied who simply return to spawning grounds inside the fisheries themselves.

For the Indians, the immense changes in the salmon's natural ways will permanently affect their subsistence. The production is also an informative reminder that the traditional Indian approach to drawing subsistence from nature benefitted not only humans, but was also in harmony with the ecology.

SAN PABLITO PAPER/EL PAPEL SAN PABLITO
For description see *Mexico Indigena Series*.

SEASONS OF A NAVAJO
1984, 60 min. Producer/camera: John Borden. Associate producer/sound: Joanna Hattery. Editor: Michel Chalufour. Research: Neil Goodwin. Narrator: Will Lyman. Produced by Peace River Films for KAET-TV, Tempe, AZ. Executive producer: Anthony Schmitz. ¾" vt. Color. In English and Navajo with English subtitles. Dist.: NAPBC/PBS.

SEASONS OF A NAVAJO documents a year in the life of Chauncey and Dorothy Neboyia. Shot in the Canyon de Chelly, on the Defiance Plateau, and close to Chinle, Arizona, the film was made by independent producers known for their careful photography of nature. The attention paid to environment and its place in the lives of the Navajo is extraordinary. For the first time on film we are shown a more authentic view of a pastoral way of life, involving traditional homesites in many different environments. The film also shows that for many younger Navajo this is a valued way of life, but one belonging to an older generation.

The Neboyias, at their tasks, speak to the filmmakers about their lives and concerns. Several aspects of Navajo life rarely seen on film are shown. It is generally known that elaborate rituals are used by the Navajo for healing by restoring harmony to the patient and the community. Throughout each day traditional Navajos also perform small rituals to maintain harmony. Chauncey is shown at prayer and at the sweat lodge.

Also filmed is the *kinaalda*, the ritual for young women which has been central to the Navajo and expresses some of the values of its matrilineal structure. In the film parts of its celebration are shown, including foot races and the blessing by the young initiate of the members of her family. The girl and her parents have come from Phoenix where they live, demonstrating the closeness of a wide circle of relatives and the value traditional elders still have for their more urbanized kinfolk.

As an exploration of the vital significance of their customs and their lands to traditional Navajos, the film is excellent. Although it indicates that the Navajo do not all live in this manner, the film evokes a sense that in each generation traditional Navajo ways will be valued for a long time to come. Possibly no image conveys this sense of continuity better than a scene in which Chauncey Neboyia sings, holding close a baby who is thus literally encircled by the rhythm of his people's tradition.

SHENANDOAH FILMS

Producers: Vern Korb and Carole Korb. Director: Carole Korb (except where noted). Camera/editor: Vern Korb. 16mm, ¾" vt, ½" (VHS, Beta). Color. Dist.: Shenandoah.

A Yurok-owned production company, Shenandoah has made numerous films, filmstrips, and slide tapes about Indian culture, particularly in northern California. The productions, intended for educational use, focus on improving the education, employment skills, and cultural pride of Indian children and youth and giving a general audience a better understanding of the continuing significance of their heritage to Native Americans. For a complete list of titles contact the distributor.

Among the productions are:

AGAIN, A WHOLE PERSON I HAVE BECOME

1985, 20 min. Narrator: Will Sampson.

This film features a Wintu medicine woman, a Karok spiritual leader, and a Tolowa headman who speak of the wisdom of the old ways and who represent their revival and preservation in the present, as they lead dances for gatherings of Indian people.

IN THE BEST INTEREST OF THE CHILD: INDIAN CHILD WELFARE ACT

1984, 20 min. Narrator: Will Sampson.

In this film, acted by nonprofessional actors, a state court decision leads to a young Indian child's removal from his home, to be placed in a non-Indian foster home. The situation is replayed, but this time it is decided to have the boy remain with his own grandfather, with support services provided by the child welfare agency. Sponsored by a California law firm, the film familiarizes its audience with the problems of foster care and the provisions of the Indian Child Welfare Act. It also encourages Native Americans to play a more active role in foster care and adoption.

OUR SONGS WILL NEVER DIE

1983, 35 min. Narrator: Juni Donahue.

Yurok, Karok, and Tolowa summer cultural camps have been established in California. Here young people work together with tribal elders, as they learn surf-fishing, fish drying, sand breadmaking, net making, Indian card games, songs, stick games, and the histories of California's Indian peoples.

THE PATH OF OUR ELDERS

1986, 20 min. Narrator: Pat Tswelmaldin. Available on video only.

Pomo elders show how traditions are passed on, demonstrating traditional song and dance and the preparation and weaving of basketry utilizing a variety of natural materials.

ROOTS TO CHERISH

1983, 30 min. Directors: Marilyn Miles and Don Mahler. Field coordinator: Joy Sundberg. Narrator: Carl Degado.

This film is intended to raise the awareness of teachers and guidance personnel to the consequences their cultural differences have for Indian students. Several Indian participants — a concerned mother, a Maidu educator, a traditional Hupa teacher — and a guidance counselor speak to this issue. Suggestions are given for changing the way academic skills are evaluated and for modifying the curriculum to improve the native students' achievement.

SHUNGNAK: A VILLAGE PROFILE

1985, 30 min. Director: Daniel Housberg. Produced by the Northwest Arctic Television Center. Executive Producer: Bob Walker. ¾" vt, ½" vt. Color. Dist.: Northwest Arctic. For additional information see NORTHWEST ARCTIC VIDEO.

This production focuses on a tiny Inupiat Eskimo community in northwest Alaska, 75 miles north of the Arctic Circle. Remote by any standard, it has nevertheless seen irrevocable changes and is in many ways a participant in American mass culture. Yet Shungnak retains the character of its people's history and identity and of their unique way of life. A well-chosen mix of speakers, including elders, local educators, and young people discuss the contrast between past and present, demonstrating a strong community commitment which holds out the promise of solutions to serious contemporary problems. In Shungnak there are high rates of alcohol and drug abuse, teen pregnancy, and suicide. The necessity of cash income for survival in the modern world poses an immense problem in a community with few jobs.

Villagers discuss their subsistence practices, still important for providing food and, judging by their comments, one of the most pleasurable aspects of life in Shungnak. As the native narrator states, traditional subsistence hunting fulfills people's needs not only nutritionally but spiritually as well. The production has scenes of the year's seasonal round. Animal life includes moose, carribou, rabbit, muskrat, migratory birds, and many kinds of fish.

In SHUNGNAK the subsistence lifestyle provides a richness of experience that the people will not easily abandon, despite the changes that have come to the village and the problems that they have brought. Another view of the same community, filmed in 1976 by the Alaska Native Heritage Film Project, is shown in FROM THE FIRST PEOPLE (see description in Volume I, p. 49).

SIKSILARMIUT

For description see *Magic in the Sky.*

SONGS IN MINTO LIFE

1985, 30 min. Producer/director: Curt Madison. Camera: Leonard Kamerling, Curt Madison, and Charlotte Yager. Produced in cooperation with the Minto Village Council. ¾" vt, ½" vt. Color. In English and Tanana Athabascan. Dist.: KYUK/NAPBC/OneWest.

An exceptional documentary explores the creativity and tradition in the songs of Tanana Indians living near Minto Flats, Alaska. Their language is only now being written down, and the recording of songs, with translations in English, is rare. The production shows activities during the four seasons, with elders singing both songs they themselves have created for various occasions and traditional *khukal'ch'leek* songs, used since ancient times. Singing is shown as important to life and the continuation of Minto ways.

At an April snow camp elders sing a song in honor of relatives and friends who died in the flu epidemic in 1923. At a July fishing camp on the Tanana River a porcupine song is sung, the singer commenting with both humor and regret that once everyone understood this kind of song, but children rarely do so anymore. An elderly women sings a song for attracting moose to the hunter. As a moose is shown fleeing into the bush, she laughs about how the song did not work when she composed it. Later in the production she sings a song made to honor her husband and describes preparing a potlatch to restore his health.

An autumn moose hunt is shown, including the butchering, explained in detail. At the hunting camp several older people sing and talk about hunting songs used before the time of the Christian missionaries, remarking that they think the present hunt has been successful because so many songs have been sung this year. The tape concludes with a scene re-enacted by two older women who composed a song while waiting for the airplane which takes people between the town of Minto Flats and other locations.

Madison is an excellent videomaker whose appreciation of the knowledge of older people and their communities' contemporary ways of life are evident throughout his works. His videotapes, guided by the interests and concerns of the people, are co-produced with native Alaskans, and include HUTEETL: KOYUKON MEMORIAL POTLATCH (see description in this volume).

SPIRIT BAY SERIES

1982–1986, 28 min. each. Producers: Eric Jordan and Paul Stephens. Directors: Paul Stephens, Eric Jordan, and Keith Leckie. Writers: Paul Stephens, Keith Leckie, Ian Moore, and Jim Henshaw. ¾" vt, ½" vt (VHS, Beta). Color. In English, French, or Ojibwa. Dist.: Beacon (US)/MLFD (Canada). Both sales only.

SPIRIT BAY is an entertainment series made by an independent production company for the Canadian Broadcasting Corporation televised in Canada, Europe, and the United States. The producers' goal is to provide a continuing series which reflects some of the reality of reserve life and debunks stereotypes about Indians. They have drawn on both professional and nonprofessional Indian and Métis actors, advisors, and production personnel, intentionally making SPIRIT BAY a training ground for Native American artists.

The series, set in the fictional community of Spirit Bay, is filmed in Macdiarmid, a community on the Rocky Bay Reserve in Ontario. It depicts a remote northern Indian community through the experiences of its children, showing a life of trap lines and fishing boats, families, friends, school, adventures, and misadventures. Like many Native Americans, the residents of Spirit Bay have adapted to white society while retaining ties to the land through trapping, fishing, and hunting, which provide its characters an anchor in the hectic flow of modern life.

The series pilot told the story of an Indian family living on their trapline in winter. Following its broadcast, the producers filmed twelve more stories, which involve the young artist, Tafia; Minnow, her big brother; Rabbit, the boy from the city; his friend, Hack; and other children in the community. The themes of the programs are uniformly appealing, but directing and acting vary. Produced in French and English versions, the first seven episodes are being translated into Ojibwa. A teacher's guide is available from the distributor.

The episodes are listed in the order of broadcast:

A TIME TO BE BRAVE

For description see individual title.

RABBIT GOES FISHING

Rabbit tries to stow away on a fishing boat to return to the city, and ends up saving a family of tourists endangered by a heavy storm.

DANCING FEATHERS

Tafia and her best friend go to their first powwow in the city, where they get lost, meet a punk teen, and, finally, dance at the powwow.

CIRCLE OF LIFE

Lenore and Ruth find the burial ground of an Indian on a haunted island. When museum officials take the bones away, Lenore and her father must recover them for burial in sacred ground.

THE BLUEBERRY BICYCLE

Elton's new bike is crushed days before a big bicycle race, and the old woman Teawash makes him a composite bicycle paid for in blueberries.

THE PRIDE OF SPIRIT BAY

Everything goes wrong in amusing ways when the children of Spirit Bay decide to sell their own "works of art" in imitation of Tafia's aunt, who is an artist. Old Bernard takes Tafia on a mystic voyage to discover the real source of inspiration for her art.

RABBIT PULLS HIS WEIGHT

Following a plane crash in the winter wilderness, Rabbit improvises a sled and drags the pilot towards town, discovering a bond between them that carries them through their ordeal.

HACK'S CHOICE

Hack's uncle comes to Spirit Bay to claim a box of family relics that have healing powers, and Hack must decide whether to help him get it.

HOT NEWS

May, an ambitious reporter, finds herself at odds with her thoughtful cousin Mavis who lives at Spirit Bay, until together they face a frightening fire.

WORDS ON A PAGE

A scholarship offer threatens a father-daughter relationship, since he fears her education will take her away from Spirit Bay forever.

WATER MAGIC

When it appears a fishing voyage is jinxed, Rabbit and Hack set out on a treacherous journey to make an offering to the lake spirits.

BIG SAVE

Coming home from a broomball tournament, the bus goes off the road. Rose saves the children from freezing by building a snow shelter.

A REAL KID

When Rabbit finds out his foster mother Annie is pregnant, he fears he will be left out of the family and tries to run away. After staying to face his problems, he learns that Annie is planning to adopt him.

STANDING ALONE

1983, 58 min. Producer/editor: Tom Daly. Director: Colin Low. Project organizer: John Spotton. Camera: Ian Elkin, Rodney Gibbons, and Simon Leblanc. Sound: Bev Davidson and Claude Hazanavicius. Produced by the National Film Board of Canada. Executive producers: Barrie Howells and Michael Scott. 16mm, ¾" vt, ½" vt. Color. Dist.: Karol Media (US rentals)/NFBC (US sales). In Canada, contact local NFBC offices.

Twenty-five years ago Pete Standing Alone was the subject of a film by Colin Low which stressed the conflicts facing a young man of the Blood tribe caught between Indian and white ways. In STANDING ALONE the portrait is continued, expanding the study of change and continuity on an Indian reserve today. Standing Alone's youth — spent as an oil rig roughneck, rodeo rider, and cowboy — and his youthful thoughts on the inevitability of his culture changing radically are referred to using selections from the earlier film.

Now middle-aged, Standing Alone lives on the Blood Indian Reserve in Alberta and is active in family and tribal affairs. Through his eyes are seen many aspects of contemporary Blood life, as the script presents his reflections on change and the preservation of tribal traditions. The film shows members of Standing Alone's family engaged in contemporary Plains Indian activites. His sons train horses, and scenes of a rodeo are included. While his wife sews and decorates dance regalia, he makes a tooled leather saddle to present to Prince Charles during a royal visit to the reserve.

Standing Alone participates in activities concerned with Blood traditions. With other leaders he visits a site of ancient stone markers, known as medicine wheels. They discuss with an archeologist both the stone monuments and some human remains, about five thousand years old, found nearby. Once an outsider to the practice of the Sun Dance, he is now learning the songs and dances for this important ceremony from a holy man. Scenes from the earlier film and additional footage of contemporary dancing are used to explain the sacred beliefs of the Blood.

The film also considers the economic and political pressures which affect Indian tribes. Mineral rights on the oil-rich reserve have been leased to outside companies, but the tribal economy has received only limited benefits. Once a member of the tribal council, Standing Alone discusses his concerns about the impact of oil sales and difficulties the tribe faces in long-range planning.

Although his own life shows that a young person, once disaffected from tribal ways, can return to become a tribal leader, Standing Alone observes that it is increasingly difficult to keep anything of the old ways and that most young people today leave the reserve for work. The film presents this contradiction, providing examples both of problems facing the tribe and a reassurance that Blood ways will continue. The endurance of the Sun Dance itself seems to guarantee that, no matter how uncertain, the future of the Blood tribe will include a deep connection to its ancient past and treasured values. Colin Low's earlier film on Standing Alone as a young man is CIRCLE OF THE SUN (Dist.: NFBC).

STAR LORE

1984, 8½ min. Producer/director: Faith Hubley. Animators: Faith Hubley and William Little-john. Score composed by Conrad Cummings. Color. 16mm, ¾" vt. Dist.: Pyramid.

In this production, award-winning film animator Faith Hubley has provided an original and visually dynamic rendering of six Native American sky myths. The lively score and drawings are based on the indigenous styles of the cultures depicted.

The stories chosen for this film include an Inuit tale of a race between Sun and Moon that leads to the separation of day from night; a Pawnee tale of measuring time against the changing position of the stars; a Maya tale of a cosmic ball game in which the Hero Twins play Death and become heavenly bodies. Also included are a Campa tale, from Peru, of the birth of the sun; a Tupi tale, from Brazil, of the star god who exceeds his powers to transform and create; and a Yahgan tale, from Tierra del Fuego, in which the Moon Lady introduces mourning customs and the dead follow the Milky Way as their path to paradise.

STICKBALL: THE LITTLE BROTHER OF WAR

For description see *Creek Nation Video.*

STICKS AND STONES, LEATHER AND BONES

For description see *Ojibway and Cree Cultural Centre Video.*

THE STRENGTH OF LIFE

1984, 26 min. Producer/director/writer/editors: Scott Swearingen, Gary Robinson, and Sheila Swearingen. ¾" vt, ½" vt. Color. Dist.: Full Circle/Creek Nation/NAPBC.

This production portrays Creek-Cherokee artist Knokovtee Scott, who has breathed new life into an ancient art form by producing exquisite jewelry made with engraved shells, its motifs based on the incised shell tradition of the mound-builder cultures of the ancient Southeast. Scott's knowledge of that tradition comes from research which began when he returned home to Oklahoma after attending the Institute of American Indian Arts in Santa Fe. He first studied pieces recovered by archeologists from the Spiro Mounds in Oklahoma, then searched out their connections to the vast civilization that had spread across the Southeast many hundreds of years ago.

The artist is seen gathering purple mussel shells from the Verdigris River. In his studio he shows how he makes his jewelry pieces and explains the meaning of their imagery. Ancient Southeast motifs, such as the four winds, continue to be significant, as are many other traditions, shown in scenes from a recent Creek Green Corn ceremony. The production includes an interview with Don Wycoff of the Oklahoma Archeological Survey who gives background for the Temple Mound culture and explains the use of several of the old pieces shown.

The producers Swearingen have also documented other Oklahoma artists. Their works include ELLA MAE BLACKBEAR (see description in this volume) and RIBBONS OF THE OSAGE, on the life and art of Georgeann Robinson. Nationally recognized for her ribbonwork, an important element of the tribe's dance clothing, Robinson played a vital role in passing on Osage traditions (Dist.: Full Circle).

SUMMER OF THE LOUCHEUX

1983, 27 min. Producer/director: Gradon McCrae. Associate Producer: Linda Rasmussen. Camera: Blake James. Sound: Lorna Rasmussen. Editors: Parajayo R. Reece and Gradon McCrae. Music: Mo Marshall. 16mm, ¾" vt, ½" vt. Color. In English or Loucheux. Dist.: New Day (US)/ Tamarack (Canada, sales only).

The Loucheux, also known as the Kutchin, are one of the northernmost Indian peoples, living in both Canada and Alaska. This film profiles the Andre family who live in Arctic Red River, a tiny community nearly one hundred miles north of the Arctic Circle, in Canada's Northwest Territories. As one of the remaining families to hunt and fish traditionally, the Andres spend several weeks each summer at their fishing camp on the Mackenzie River.

SUMMER OF THE LOUCHEUX focuses on 28-year-old Alestine Andre who works with her father to catch fish and process and preserve them for use in winter, and who teaches Loucheux skills to the young niece who has accompanied them. Alestine narrates the beautifully filmed scenes of day-to-day life, reflecting on the importance of family life and the meaning she finds in following traditional Loucheux ways.

When the Andres visit Alestine's 93-year-old grandmother, the past traditions and history of the Loucheux are evoked. One of the few Loucheux who have remained isolated from town life, she lives in a log cabin near the river. Her account of life as a young woman, accompanied by archival photographs, recreates a picture of the annual subsistence cycle as it was followed at the turn of the century. By sharing their experiences, two generations of this family — Alestine and her grandmother — provide a rarely heard woman's perspective on Native American life. Through their two accounts, the film becomes a subtle portrait of culture change and the continuing strength of Loucheux traditions.

THE SUN DAGGER

1982, 60 min. or 30 min. Producer/writer: Anna Sofaer. Director/editor: Albert Ihde. Camera: Robert Kaylor and Karl Kernberger. Narrator: Robert Redford. 16mm, ¾" vt, ½" vt. Color. Dist.: Bullfrog.

Evidence of a unique calendrical marker at Fajada Butte in Chaco Canyon, New Mexico, has been accumulated since 1977 by artist Anna Sofaer. Replete with ruins today, Chaco Canyon was populated a thousand years ago by agriculturalists, known as the Anasazi, who are probably the ancestors of some of today's Pueblo peoples. Their apartment complexes and ritual kivas, road and irrigation systems, and skillfully made objects of ceramic and weaving indicate that they inhabited a complex society organized for stability.

The film recounts Sofaer's discovery of two spiral petroglyphs and her growing conviction, based on observing a pointer of light, or "sun dagger," that the butte was the ancient site of an astronomical observatory. It follows the progress of her investigation as she marshals the resources, including skillfull co-workers, to explore the site and interpret its significance to the ancient culture of Chaco Canyon.

Sofaer's findings have generated controversy within the field of academic archaeoastronomy. The film skillfully underscores her claim that the dispute about her findings shows an ethnocentric bias in academia which implies that cultures of native North America were unable to utilize sophisticated calendrical systems. For academics, at issue is the place of the devoted amateur's findings within the scholarly world, and whether an individual's passionate researches are adequately objective to produce true insights into the past.

TESHUINADA

For description see *Maria Sabina: Mujer Espiritu.*

THEY NEVER ASKED OUR FATHERS

1982, 58 min. Producer/writer: Corey Flintoff. Director/editor: John A. McDonald. Camera: Alexie Isaac and John A. McDonald. Narrator: John Active. Produced by KYUK-TV, Bethel, AK. All video formats. Color. In English and Yup'ik with English subtitles. Dist.: KYUK. For additional information see KYUK VIDEO.

Nunivak Island, twenty miles from the mainland of southwest Alaska, is rich in wildlife. For two thousand years it has served as home and hunting grounds for the Yup'ik Eskimo who live there. Today most of the island belongs to the federal government for use as a national wildlife refuge. Through interviews and scenes of various aspects of Yup'ik life on Nunivak, this videotape presents the situation of a native people whose daily affairs are dominated by the federal government located thousands of miles away.

Speaking in Yup'ik, hunters tell of their nomadic past and caribou hunting, and of the beginnings of their year-round village and reindeer herding. By 1930 a portion of the island had been set aside as a federal bird refuge. That year, without consulting the islanders, musk ox herds were imported from Greenland. Gradually, through outside intervention, less and less land was available for subsistence.

When the Alaska Native Claims Settlement Act was passed, most communities in Alaska were able to select their own traditional lands for ownership. But because of the numerous wildlife reserves on Nunivak Island, lands twenty miles away on the mainland were assigned to the community. As they discuss their concerns, several people express dissatisfaction with the way government involvement has severely constricted their way of life, which depends on access to the land. Since the time of their fathers, the Nunivak Islanders say, they have not been consulted about any of the many changes imposed on them.

THROUGH THIS DARKEST NIGHT

1986, 12 min. Producer: Susan Malins. Director: Daniel Salazar. Writer: Linda Ferguson. Camera: Maxine Stadnik and Daniel Salazar. Advisors and narrators: Vivian Locust, Richard Peters, Rick Alcott. Produced for the Denver Art Museum. Project director: Gretchen Johnson. ¾" vt, ½" vt (VHS, Beta). Dist.: ADL/DAM (both sales only).

This videotape was originally produced for installation in "A Persistent Vision: Art of the Reservation Days," an exhibition at the Denver Art Museum, curated by Richard Conn. The scripted narration presents Indian people's experiences during the early reservation period, including some drawn from period accounts.

Three Native American speakers provide the first-person accounts in sequence. A man speaks of the upheaval experienced when the buffalo were finally gone and his family was compelled to move to the reservation. A woman describes how she used her strength and traditional skills to ensure that her family and people would survive on the reservation. The third speaker tells of being sent to boarding school and the isolation and humiliation of that experience for an

Indian youth. Archival photographs, views of objects in the exhibition, and footage of the environment of the Plains are skillfully woven together.

Director Daniel Salazar has interviewed a number of native philosophers of North America and Mexico in ANCIENT SPIRIT, LIVING WORD: THE ORAL TRADITION (Dist.: NAPBC).

A TIME TO BE BRAVE

1982, 28 min. Producer/editor: Eric Jordan. Director/writer: Paul Stephens. Associate producer: Lena Nabigon. Camera: Naohika Kurita. Sound: Jim Robinson. Production manager: Sally Dundas. Opening song: Buffy Sainte-Marie. Consultant: Shirley Cheechoo. Cast: Tafia — Cynthia Debassige; Baba — Ron Cook; Minnow — Eugene Thompson; Gok'mis — Kate Assiniwe. 16mm, ¾" vt, ½" vt. Color. Dist.: Beacon. For additional information see SPIRIT BAY SERIES.

Filmed on location in Ontario, this pilot episode of a television series focuses on the Shibagabo family—Tafia, her older brother Minnow, their grandmother Gok'mis, and their father Baba—living on their trapline in winter. The roles are acted by a cast of professional and nonprofessional Ojibwa actors. The plot is concerned with the growth of young Tafia, living at home, and Minnow, who is in boarding school and yearns to be with his family. As the story opens Minnow runs away from school, but his father persuades him to return to gain more book learning to add to his knowledge of the bush.

Scenes of the family at home and of tracking and trapping establish a good sense of daily life. The children's mother has died and Baba shows his concern for them by giving each a momento that represents the continued closeness of their family. Tafia also finds comfort in painting, making works in a recognizable Ojibwa style. Additional issues arise. A white man, ignorant of their ways, comes to obtain an agreement to lease tree cutting rights, which the father decides to refuse. When her father is seriously injured in an accident, Tafia must decide to swallow her fear of the train, which took her mother away to die in a remote hospital, and flag it down to get help.

This is a well-acted and crafted drama. One of the best episodes of the series, it presents positive views of Indian life in settings that native and non-native children will be able to identify with. A TIME TO BE BRAVE conveys an authentic sense of a northern Indian environment and shows the nature of family caring that enables maturing children to make hard choices.

TO PUT AWAY THE GODS

1982, 90 min. Producer/directors: Brian Huberman, Ed Hugetz, and Michael Rees. 8mm film transferred to ¾" vt. Color. Dist.: Huberman.

This videotape documents the process of culture change in the Lacandon Maya village of Naha' in the Mexican state of Chiapas. It examines how traditional leadership is being replaced by new patterns which stem from the presence of government and development interests in the Lacandon rain forest of southern Mexico.

The elder Chan K'in demonstrates and discusses his knowledge of the Lacandon tradition. He and his friend Mateo note that there is no one of the younger generation who can continue this kind of spiritual and traditional leadership. Running parallel to these conversations is a series of events concerned with the selection of a *presidente* from the younger men. The presidente's job is an administrative creation of the Mexican government to facilitate its dealings with tribal people. The significance of the office stems from the fact that the presidente becomes the intermediary between the community and the world outside.

This type of leadership has no precedent in Lacandon tradition. For example, in their own community people try to avoid expressing or even being exposed to anger. But since the presidente has contact with the outside world which denigrates the Lacandon, the office-holder is inevitably exposed to conflict. He also controls Lacandon resources which come from the outside, such as cash payments and use of the community's truck, provided by the lumber company which logs mahogany trees on community lands.

During the time of filming, the older son of Chan K'in is serving as presidente. He speaks openly about abandoning the old ways. Chan K'in's younger son is chosen for the position when his brother, sensing the community's dissatisfaction, resigns. Although more sympathetic to traditional ways, the younger son has not learned the old rituals, songs, or body of religious myths that his father knows, nor does he wish to continue as presidente. In fact, there seems to be no young man well-equipped for the demands of this office because it is so culturally uncongenial to the Lacandon. It is one change among many that the people will continue to face.

Members of the community are shown watching scenes of the film and commenting on them, and the filmmakers interact with them, asking questions and making observations about how old ways are being confronted by new ones. As traditional leadership and traditional means for making community decisions are being abandoned, it is uncertain what can guarantee the continuation of this Maya way of life.

TODOS SANTOS CUCHUMATAN: REPORT FROM A GUATEMALAN VILLAGE

1982, 41 min. Producer/director/writer: Olivia Carrescia. Camera: Vicente Galindez. Sound: Michael Penland. Editors: Olivia Carrescia and Robert Rosen. 16mm, ¾" vt. Color. In Spanish with English voice-over and narration. Dist.: Icarus.

Todos Santos, a Mayan village in the Cuchumatan mountains of western Guatemala, has been accessible by road only since 1965. Surrounded by ranchos and hamlets without electricity, the village is typical of many communities of Indian farmers in southern Mexico and Central America. Their ancient culture is rich in tradition and custom, and they are distinguished from other villagers in their region by their clothing, language, and patron saint.

The film opens by noting that half the population of Guatemala, predominantly rural and rapidly increasing, is Maya. The Indians live in a culture separate from and largely misunderstood by both their non-Indian countrymen and North Americans. They also have scant access to the country's economic resources. One of the more pointed observations in the film is that in Guatemala "65 percent of the arable land is owned by 2 percent of the population, mostly the military."

In Todos Santos the twelve thousand inhabitants grow their own crops on small farms, which no longer provide enough for their survival. As a result, most of the men and many young women are forced to work in far-off coastal areas as poorly paid migrant workers, picking cotton, coffee, or fruit. Although people in the film describe the many hardships of this seasonal migration, they also value the income which helps them survive and which provides the funds for the proper celebration of the community fiesta. Men, women, and children in this austere setting seem determined to make a good life for themselves. However, the film raises the question of how they can cope with the changes to village and family life which the migration is causing.

A major segment of the film is devoted to the annual fiesta celebrated at the beginning of November. The observation of rituals, ritual horse races, and very heavy consumption of alcohol are shown as aspects of the celebration. The film provides insight into the changing conditions which are increasing the difficulties of an already arduous lifestyle in the 1960's and 1970's. Although migrant labor has become a fact of economic life, the villagers are quietly aware of the toll it takes. Although the film does not document the political conflict which began to engulf this area within a month following its filming, it clearly describes basic inequalities facing the villagers.

TRADITIONAL INUPIAT ESKIMO HEALTH SERIES
For description see *Northwest Arctic Video.*

TRADITIONAL INUPIAT ESKIMO TECHNOLOGY SERIES
For description see *Northwest Arctic Video.*

THE TRADITIONAL MIGRATION
For description see *KYUK Video.*

THE TRADITIONAL SNOWSHOE
For description see *Ojibway and Cree Cultural Centre Video.*

TREATY 8 COUNTRY
1982, 44 min. Producer/directors: Anne Cubitt and Hugh Brody. Camera: Jim Bizzochi. Editors: Justine Dancy and Anne Cubitt. 16mm (sales and rentals); ¾" vt, ½" vt (sales only). Color. Dist.: CFDW.

This film was made in response to the growing concern of Indian people in northwest Canada over the abrogation of their treaty rights. It documents subsistence hunting of the Beaver Indians of the Halfway River Band in northeast British Columbia, and records their views on their current situation. Treaty 8 was signed in the years between 1899 and 1915 by various bands of the Beaver, Cree, Slavey, and Chipewayan. Although the Indians ceded their aboriginal territory, they retained rights to hunt, fish, and trap there, with the understanding these rights would never be extinguished. Settlement and mining has proceeded throughout the twentieth century and has only recently threatened this provision. Intensified resource development, heralded by the Alaskan oil pipeline which crosses their hunting area, now threatens to destroy these peoples' way of life.

The sparsity of explanatory narration provides both the film's weakest and its strongest points. The hunters' comments on Treaty 8 history and their present difficulty do not fully explain the issues involved, and may be confusing, especially to viewers in the United States. What these rights mean to the people, however, is clearly conveyed through the presentation of daily life in a summer hunting camp. Traditionally, the Beaver relied almost entirely on animals for food, and hunting is still vital. As one hunter explains, "We depend on meat. If we try to live like white people, we'll go hungry." Using horses, the men hunt moose, butcher the animal, and return to camp. As they relax, the women and girls cut up and dry the meat. Scenes of informal camp life, traditional dance, and children accompanying trappers to set rabbit snares, show how important this way of life is to their survival, both physical and cultural.

TRUST FOR NATIVE AMERICAN CULTURES AND CRAFTS VIDEO

Producer/narrator/editor: Todd Crocker. Director/writer/camera/editor: Henri Vaillancourt. Second camera: Bryan Hopkins. ¾" vt, ½" vt. Color. In English and native languages. Dist.: Trust.

The purpose of the Trust for Native American Cultures and Crafts is to document aspects of the material culture of northern Native Americans. Working in Eastern Canada, the Trust has accomplished a major task in preserving a record of the skills traditionally passed on from generation to generation which are now threatened by changes throughout the North.

The productions record processes of making traditional crafts, from the selection of raw materials to the completion and use of the finished objects. Closeups and natural lighting are used to good advantage. The tapes record directly, with ambient sound and conversation in native languages between the family members who work together, and are filmed on location. A simple explanation in English follows the showing of each stage in the process.

The people filmed seem at ease before the camera, a credit to the tact and responsiveness of the producers. One participant who was initially reluctant to be filmed agreed when, acknowledging that the young people are not learning these skills, she decided that the videotapes would allow her to pass on to her grandchildren a record of the things she values. Commenting on what some of the participants think of their project, one of the producers described what is basic to the tapes. "They know we're doing it because we really value what they are doing."

BEAVERTAIL SNOWSHOES *(1981, 40 min.)*

Sam Rabbitskin and his family, who live in Quebec near Mistassini Lake, are shown constructing traditional Cree Indian beavertail snowshoes. Steps in the process include tree selection and cutting, splitting and stave construction, measuring and bending the frame, final shaping of the frames, cutting of the *babiche*, and weaving of the toe, tail, and middle sections of the snowshoe.

BUILDING AN ALGONQUIN BIRCHBARK CANOE *(1984, 57 min.)*

In 1980, at Manawaki, Quebec, Jocko Carle and Basil Smith built birchbark canoes so the process could be videotaped. Archival photographs and film introduce the documentation of this method of canoe building, opening with selection of raw materials, showing stages of construction, and concluding with the two artisans using the finished canoes. Although the historical narration is wordy, the filming of the building process is interesting and thorough.

INDIAN HIDE TANNING *(1981, 35 min.)*

For the Cree of northern Quebec, moose and caribou are valuable as food and for the materials they supply for making the articles people need. In this tape all steps necessary for cleaning, tanning, and smoking a large hide and the use of the hide in the manufacture of moccasins and of snowshoes are shown. Individuals filmed include members of the Matoush family, Sarah Bosum, Sophie Coon, and Anna Trapper.

TULE TECHNOLOGY: NORTHERN PAIUTE USES OF MARSH RESOURCES IN WESTERN NEVADA

1983, 42 min. Producer: Thomas Vennum, Jr. Narrator: Louella George. Consultants: Margaret Wheat and Catherine Fowler. Produced for the Smithsonian Folklife Studies Monograph/Film Series. 16mm, ¾" vt, ½" vt. Color. Dist.: PSU.

Northern Paiute Indian peoples have lived near the Stillwater marshes of western Nevada for generations, depending for subsistence on fish, waterfowl, and eggs, and using tule reeds and cattails to manufacture tools and shelter. TULE TECH-NOLOGY shows a number of traditional uses of tule as Wuzzie George and members of her family and friends construct a number of Northern Paiute artifacts. They tie tule together to make a small boat to be poled through the marsh water for duck hunting and gathering weaving materials. They also twine a duck egg bag, weave a duck decoy, and construct a cattail house.

The film's narration is provided by Mrs. George's son and granddaughter, and includes reminiscences of many aspects of traditional Paiute life that have disappeared. As can be the case with amateur narrators, sometimes the sound track is difficult to understand, but the film's description of little-known native technologies is invaluable. The film was shot at two different time periods, 1964 and 1978–1979, and the finished film was released in 1983.

As part of a series produced by the Smithsonian Institute's Folklife Progam (see THE DRUMMAKER in Volume I, p. 40), this film is complemented by a monograph of the same title by Catherine Fowler.

TURTLE SHELLS

For description see *Creek Nation Video*.

THE 21ST ANNUAL WORLD ESKIMO-INDIAN OLYMPICS

1983, 27 min. Producer/director/camera/editor: Skip Blumberg. Sound/lighting: Jan Kroeze. Post-production engineer: John J. Godfrey. Produced for the PBS series Matters of Life and Death. *Executive producer: Carol Brandenburg. ¾" vt, ½" vt. Color. Dist. Dist.: EAI.*

For centuries native people of the Arctic have gathered to compete in games of skill. Based on this tradition, the World Eskimo-Indian Olympics have been held as an organized event in Fairbanks, Alaska, since 1961. During the three-day gathering in 1982 more than ten thousand fans filled the stands to see competitive events based on the skills, strengths, and endurance important in the traditional Eskimo and northern Indian way of life. Such contests as the two-foot and one-foot high kicks, seal-skinning contests, knuckle hop, and blanket toss are among the more than fifty events held.

For both native villagers and urban dwellers, the games provide a living connection to their traditions and are a focus of cultural pride. The feeling of cooperation and mutual support is expressed in every aspect of the occasion. Though all try their hardest, no one at the games takes the competition too seriously. The tape's lively and skillfully edited portrayal of the events is heightened by portraits of two Inupiat Eskimo athletes. Reggie Joule is seen in his work at an Inupiat skills summer camp and Carol Pickett, filmed in her home, speaks with the videomaker about the importance to her, as a young urban woman, of her Eskimo heritage. ESKIMO-INDIAN OLYMPICS, offering fast-paced coverage, is by an award-winning video artist known for documenting unique and entertaining sports.

UTE INDIAN TRIBE VIDEO

Producer/director of all programs: Larry Cesspooch. Clay animator: Urshel Tohannie. ¾" vt, ½" vt. Color. Dist.: Ute Indian Tribe.

Since 1979, the Ute Indian Tribe has been documenting Ute traditions and tribal concerns on video, with subjects ranging from drying deer meat to Ute-language instructional tapes. The Audio-Visual program works in cooperation with the Ute Language, Culture, and Traditions Committee, a decision-making body for cultural issues and information, on the Uintah and Ouray Ute Reservation, located at Fort Duchesne, Utah. More than 125 tapes are currently in the tribe's archives. For information about titles and about production services offered, contact the distributor.

NOOdtVWEEP/UTE INDIAN LAND *(1986, 18 min.)*

This videotape on Ute Indian history begins with the Ute legend of the creation of the land. The production goes on to describe the process by which the Ute, originally living in Wyoming, Utah, Colorado, and the Four Corners area of New Mexico, lost their lands in the nineteenth century. In 1890, following the discovery of gold, several bands were removed from Colorado to the Uintah Reservation (now the Uintah and Ouray Ute Reservation). The production includes interviews, historical photographs, and other historical materials to illustrate this decisive period in Ute history.

UTE BEAR DANCE STORY *(1983, 15 min.)*

This videotape opens with Bear Dance chief Henry Cesspooch telling his grandson the story of the origin of the Bear Dance, an important ceremony held each spring on Ute lands. Charming animation using clay figures re-creates the story, and archival footage of the dance brings to life the ceremony as it is done by contemporary Ute people.

A VIOLATION OF TRUST

1982, 26 min. Producer/director: Bill Jersey. Producer/writer: Jim Belson. Camera: Robin Hirsch. Sound: John Morrell and Jaime Kibben. Editor: Frank Cervarich. Narrator: Jerry Landis. ¾" vt. Color. Dist.: Catticus.

For description see *Voices of Native Americans*.

VOICES OF NATIVE AMERICANS

1983, 58 min. Producer: Audrey Barnes. Writer/host: Diane Wildman. Camera: Thomas Brown and Martin Kos. Aspen conference — producer/director: Don Grissom. Camera: Alvin Allen, Bob Waybright, and Don Grissom. Editor: Robert Henninger. California conference — see credits for A VIOLATION OF TRUST. All video formats. Color. Dist.: TWN.

This is an absorbing look at the different approaches to current problems being taken by Native American leaders in the United States. A documentation of two conferences, the program opens with a presentation of the background for the meetings. It notes that the budgetary cutbacks of the present federal government have taken a toll on Indian people and that current policy is to provide less money for tribal needs, expecting corporate contributions and tribal economic development to make the difference.

The first conference, on tradition and modernization, was held for two weeks at the Aspen Institute in Colorado. The participants are successful native leaders in government, business, health, and cultural life in the United States. They speak frankly among themselves of questions of identity and of the difficulties they think their peoples face in upcoming years. They see current federal policy which seeks to reduce tribes' dependence on government support as posing a threat to the continued existence of the tribes and as destructive of what they, as leaders much in contact with mainstream America, see as most valuable about native life.

Participants include moderator Jamake Highwater; lawyer David Harrison (Osage); psychiatric nurse Phyllis Old Dog Cross (Mandan/Hidatsa); Assistant Secretary, Department of the Interior, Roy Sampsel (Choctaw); businessman David Powless (Oneida); and president of Americans for Indian Opportunity, LaDonna Harris (Comanche).

The second gathering, held in 1982 in Deganawidah-Quetzalcoatl University in northern California, presents a more politically radical native leadership. This segment of the program is available as a separate production (see A VIOLATION OF TRUST above). The conference, called the American Indian International Tribunal by its organizers, indicts the United States government for its violation of trust relationships guaranteed by treaties. American Indian activists forcefully articulate their aims and goals. Issues addressed include dependency, harmful government interference, and the problem of tribespeople who sell their "Indianness" for profit.

Among the participants who speak for the reinstitution of the ancient wisdom and sovereignty of their cultures are elders and younger leaders, such as Bob Gregory (Inupiat Eskimo), the late Philip Deere (Muscogee Creek), Oren Lyons (Onondaga), Janet McCloud (Tulalip-Duwamish), Dennis Banks (Ojibwa), and Matthew King (Oglala Sioux). This segment shows that Native American concerns have much in common with issues facing other indigenous people in the world and that an active leadership can focus on these common concerns for greater political strength.

WALKING WITH GRANDFATHER *and* GREAT WOLF AND LITTLE MOUSE SISTER

1983. 26 min. Producer/director: Phil Lucas. Story: Lionel Kinuwa. Illustrator: Patricia Lane. Writer/editor: Philip N. Lane, Jr. Editor/music: Mark Hoover. Produced by the Four Worlds Project, University of Lethbridge, Alberta, Canada. Executive producer: Philip N. Lane, Jr. Slides transferred to ¾" vt, ½" vt. Color animation. Dist.: Four Worlds (Canada)/PLP (US).

The University of Lethbridge is developing curriculum materials and sponsoring events to bring native people together to work on community development and to eliminate substance abuse. In its Department of Education, the Four Worlds Project has completed production of the first of an animated series of Indian legends told through slides.

In the introductory segment, the storyteller Joshua Low Dog teaches two children who are studying ecology in school that nature itself has wisdom to share with those who are able to learn. In the tale Great Wolf has lost his eyes and asks for help from Little Mouse Sister who willingly gives him her own eyes. Great Wolf takes her to the sacred lake to ask help for her from the Great Spirit, and on the way they encounter other species—Otter, Coyote, Horned Owl. The Great Spirit rewards Little Mouse Sister, transforming her into Eagle, an enduring symbol of love, understanding, and compassion. The story, simple yet strong, combines charming illustrations, shown as separate frames, and a good script. The characters' voices, performed by native readers, are pleasant and expressive.

Among Native American filmmaker Phil Lucas' productions is the series IMAGES OF INDIANS, which explores Hollywood stereotypes (for description see Volume I, p. 58–59). Several recent productions have been concerned with recovery from the devastating effects of alcoholism, including WHERE WE'VE BEEN AND WHERE WE'RE GOING (Dist.: Four Worlds (Canada)/PLP (US)); a series, THE HONOUR OF ALL, has been produced for the Alkali Lake Indian Band of British Columbia (Dist.: PLP).

THE WAY OF THE DEAD INDIANS/LE CHEMIN DES INDIENS MORTS

1983, 90 min. Producer/directors: Michel Perrin and Jean Arlaud. Camera: Jean Arlaud. Sound: Philippe Senechal. Editor: C. Boigeol. Produced by the Centre National de la Recherche Scientifique Audiovisuel, France. 16mm transferred to ¾" vt. Color. In French, Spanish and Guajiro with English subtitles. Dist.: FACSEA.

This ethnographic film documents the place of mythology in the past and present lives of the Guajiro Indians, a tribe of one hundred thousand people living in a desert peninsula on the Venezuela-Colombia border, about sixty miles from the port city of Maracaibo. Ethnographer Michel Perrin had already done seven years of field research before returning to make this production. It focuses on the friends and members of the family of Isho, from whom the Guajiro myths which thread through the film had been recorded by Perrin before the elder's death.

The film opens with a funeral, perhaps a symbol for the burial of Isho. The narration focuses on Guajiro beliefs as revealed in their mythological tradition. Included are tales told by villagers at home and recited in a more elegiac manner by a narrator as various Guajiro activities are shown. Since the myths deal with the meaning of life and death, funeral rituals provide the film's dominant metaphor for Guajiro cosmology. The living, connected to the dead through ancestry and ritual, will one day join them on the path which leads safely to the afterlife, the "way of dead Indians."

The continuity offered by traditional ways is contrasted with the effects of present-day changes. Brief scenes in Maracaibo show the conditions under which many of the twenty thousand who have immigrated there now live. In a lengthy segment some return home to observe a "second funeral," the memorial ceremony held some years after a death in which the remains are reburied and mourning ends. These scenes concerned with reburial are filmed aesthetically and resonate with the filmmaker's fascination with the funerary practices. The viewer is unable to judge if this also reflects the Guajiro's perception of their ritual.

The film lacks a structure sufficient for exploring fully the numerous themes it presents. The absence of any central Guajiro participants and the use of voice-over narrative create a feeling of distance in the viewer. Despite these flaws, its excellent photography and its presentation of ritual and mythology at various levels make this a documentary of great interest. Ultimately, the film is concerned with the dying out of Guajiro culture. In its final scene, in which a child is teaching his parents how to write, it suggests that the oral tradition which has given context to all Guajiro life is itself on the edge of absolute change.

A WEAVE OF TIME

1986, 60 min. Producers: Susan Fanshel with John Adair and Deborah Gordon. Director: Susan Fanshel. Camera: Robert Achs and Jack Parsons. Sound: Michael Penland and Jack Loefler. Editors: Susan Fanshel and Deborah Gordon. 16mm, ¾" vt (sales only), ½" vt (sales and rentals). Black-and-white and color. Dist.: Direct Cinema.

This film follows the lives of four generations of the Burnsides, a Navajo family from the Pine Springs community in Arizona on the Navajo reservation. In 1938 anthropologist John Adair lived with this family and filmed their daily activities and artistic techniques. Forty-five years and three generations later, director Susan Fanshel returned with him and created a film which incorporates Adair's footage, providing a rare opportunity to explore many aspects of change in Navajo life.

Although the film opens with a ritual house warming, the house is a new frame house, and the Navajo chants are followed by the Catholic priest's blessing. By focusing on a middle-aged couple, it not only pursues how change has affected traditional Navajo ways, but also how people change as they mature. Isabel Burnside and her husband Daniel Deschinny are not used by the film to represent either "Navajo-ness" or the problems of traditions in change, but throughout are seen as individuals.

For Isabel, contributing to the family income as a weaver now seems less important than her pursuit of a college degree. For her husband Daniel, shown in his work as a tribal lawyer, maturity has brought a deepening interest in Navajo spiritual ways. He studies with his wife's uncle to learn the intricate songs and knowledge of a traditional singer. By documenting this couple's efforts to bridge the gap between their culture's values and the demands that modern life makes upon them, the film portrays with authenticity the complexity of Indian people's lives today.

The recollections of the older generation—of John Adair's friends John Burnside and his sister, the weaver Mabel Burnside (who is Isabel's mother)— are juxtaposed with the next generation's observations and experiences. A WEAVE OF TIME is a subtle and compelling documentary, unusual in its refusal to romanticize its participants and committed to a clear view of people who are secure in the strength of their cultural traditions even as they change.

WHEN THE MOUNTAINS TREMBLE

1983, 83 min. Producer/editor: Peter Kinoy. Director/camera: Thomas Sigel. Director/sound: Pamela Yates. Original music: Ruben Blades. 16mm. Color. Dist.: New Yorker.

Concerned with documenting the recent brutal conflict in Guatemala, this film presents the view of the people of the rural highlands who have most suffered in it. Although filmmakers Yates and Sigel document both sides, traveling with both the army and the guerrillas, the film shows that the root cause of suppression in Guatemala lies in the overwhelming involvement of American interests in its political history. Most of it is narrated by Rigoberta Menchu, a 23-year-old Quiché Maya woman who is a spokesperson for the guerrilla umbrella group, Guatemalan National Revolutionary Unity. The film makes a strong visual impact as Menchu, seated before a stark black background and dressed in her classic and richly colored Quiché clothing, speaks eloquently. This interview testifies to both her rural Mayan identity and her political awareness. She traces her politicization, describing atrocities against her family and other villagers committed by the army.

As the film opens, staged scenes present the CIA-led coup of 1954, in support of an American concern, the United Fruit Company, which removed the first democratically-elected president from office. This earlier event sets the background for the excesses of the later governments which are described in the production. Although an inventive method for presenting past reality and perhaps a comment on the selective nature of filmed reality in documentaries, the opening remains somewhat isolated from the rest of the film.

In some ways the messages of the film are delivered more effectively in its informal moments, particularly in the horrifying eyewitness accounts of atrocities and the scenes with soldiers who have committed them, they believe, in the line of duty to their country. Since the film was made for audiences in the United States, it focuses on the ways American involvement in Guatamela has helped sustain the oppressive conditions. In one sequence, then-president General Rios Montt, who headed the country during its bloodiest period, is filmed attending a revival meeting of the American-led evangelical Church of God.

WHEN THE MOUNTAINS TREMBLE experiments with several cinema conventions to make a documentary of unusual interest. Although somewhat polemical, the film leaves its audience with a forceful analysis of how repression in Guatemala has affected its Indian population and what have been its political causes. The filmmakers have also produced a videotape, GUATEMALA PERSONAL TESTIMONIES, in which the Indians of several villages describe the atrocities they have experienced (Dist.: Icarus).

WHERE WE'VE BEEN AND WHERE WE'RE GOING
For description see *Walking With Grandfather.*

WHISTLE IN THE WIND
1982–1984, 16 min. Producer/director: Anne Makepeace. Camera: Dennis Irwin. Sound: Blair Dickinson. Narrators: Carlos Baron and Oswaldo Villazon. Music: Los Payadores. Actors: Huascar—Rene Aguirre; Inti—Gonzalo Aguirre. 16 mm ¾" vt, ½" vt. Color. In Spanish or English. Dist.: FI.

Myths and legends of the Aymara Indians of highland Bolivia provide the basis for this tale of a boy's sacrifice to the gods of the Andes. The tale is concerned with the boy Inti, his father Huascar, and his pet llama Mayta, who live just above a small tin mining town. An earthquake has destroyed most of the village. Huascar, a shaman, knowing that the mountain spirit Apu demands a sacrifice before the villagers can live there in safety, decides to offer Mayta. When the boy tries to save his pet and appease the god himself, he is the one who is taken as the sacrifice.

The legend is concerned with Aymara appreciation of sacrifice and belief in the importance and, ultimately, the sacredness of the spirits of human heroes who protect the living. Inti, a charming little boy in the film, is also a culture hero of this type, whose sacrifice is for the greater good of both his people and the llama herds on which their lives depend. The story also emphasizes the importance of sacred places to Native Americans, showing the Andes as the dwelling place of gods and the spirits of heroes whose presence is often marked by impressive natural rock formations and waterways.

The parts are acted by a Bolivian musician living in the United States and his real-life son. In the segments which present them as a contemporary Indian father and son, the father suggests that the spirit of the Andes, commemorated in tales like this, continues to stay alive in contemporary descendants of the ancient Aymara.

WITH THE SOUL BETWEEN THE TEETH
For description see *Mexico Indigena Series.*

XOCHIMILCO
For description see *Mexico Indigena Series.*

XUNAN (THE LADY)
1983, 90 min. Producer/directors: Margrit Keller and Peter von Gunter. 16mm. Color. For distribution information contact: Keller.

This portrait focuses on a remarkable woman living in the State of Chiapas in southern Mexico. Gertrude Dolby Blom not only pursues the cause of the Lacandon rain forest's preservation and of the Maya Indians who inhabit it, but also makes photographs and runs the Na Balom Foundation in San Cristobal de las Casas. In this role she has served as doyenne for countless scholars, filmmakers, and visitors to the Maya communities of the area. The film is shot in a cinema verité style which permits a view of many aspects of Blom's life and helps define her strong personality.

In the film, commentary is elicited from a wide range of people, including workers in her household, devoted volunteers, and loggers in the rain forest. The most vivid commentary, however, is given by the Lacandon elder Chan K'in, like Blom born in 1901, who has known "The Lady" since they were young adults.

Development, especially logging, has had a complex impact on the ecology of the forest and the Indian inhabitants. The Lacandon Maya, for example, now receive cash payments for the use of their traditional lands for lumbering. But for Blom and Chan K'in these benefits are far outweighed by losses that will become clearer in the long-run. For example, as roads make the mahogany forests available for cutting, they will make the Indians increasingly accessible to a wide range of outsiders, including tourists and settlers fleeing economically depressed areas of Mexico. Having seen young Lacandons become acculturated, Chan K'in is concerned that after his death no one will take care of the traditions.

Blom speaks of her impressions of the people with whom her life has been bound: "The Lacandons are perhaps the only true free people I ever came across. They led an independent life, dispersed throughout the forest. No one ever ordered them to do anything and they had never worked for anyone. Nobody could order them around . . . Chan K'in is aware of what is happening in the forest, this forest in which he and his ancestors lived, in whose cities he prays to his gods. The forest is being destroyed. Sadly he says that when the forest goes he will also go."

YUPIIT YURARYARAIT/A DANCING PEOPLE

1983, 28 min. Producer/writer/sound: Corey Flintoff. Director/camera/editor: Alexie Isaac. Writer/sound/narrator: Lillian McGill. Produced by KYUK-TV, Bethel, AK. All video formats. Color. In Yup'ik and English. Dist.: KYUK. For additional information see KYUK VIDEO.

"We are the Yupiit, the Inuit of the great river deltas and the sea. We are a dancing people." In alternating stanzas of Yup'ik Eskimo and English, this program documents a festival in the Yukon River village of St. Mary's, Alaska. Dancers from nine Yup'ik villages came together for three days at the time of freeze-up in a lively traditional dance festival, the largest to be held in decades. The gathering is one of many recent activities undertaken by Yup'ik communities to revitalize the traditional aspects of their culture. Dancing groups perform both storytelling and humorous dances. Food preparation contests and a giveaway are also shown.

   The production communicates the warmth, humor, and skill of the participants, and the pleasure the festival is giving to them and to the audience. One of many documentaries produced by KYUK-TV, and directed by a Yup'ik Eskimo videomaker, YUPIIT YURARYARAIT reflects the station's commitment to coverage of Yup'ik events and perspectives in its productions.

SUBJECTS

AGRICULTURE
See Subsistence

ANIMATIONS
Animations from Cape
  Dorset
Emergence
Letter from an Apache
Popol Vuh
Star Lore
Ute Tribe Video (series)

**ARCHEOLOGY/
  PREHISTORY**
The Longest Trail
Lost in Time
Rock Art Treasures
Spirit Bay (series)
Standing Alone
The Strength of Life
The Sun Dagger

**ART AND ARTISTS—
  CONTEMPORARY**
The Enchanted Arts
Folklore of the Muscogee
  Creek
Hopi
In Our Language
Jaune Quick-to-See Smith
Living Traditions
Parlez-Vous Yup'ik?
Revival
Robert Davidson
Siksilarmiut
Spirit Bay (series)
The Strength of Life

**ART AND ARTISTS—
  TRADITIONAL**
Also see Crafts and
  Techniques
By the Work of Our
  Hands
Ella Mae Blackbear

Eyes of the Spirit
From Hand to Hand
Hopi
Lakota Quillwork
Living Traditions
Magic Windows
Music and Dance of the
  Mohawk
Our Lives in Our Hands
Revival
Robert Davidson
A Weave of Time

**CEREMONIES AND
  RITUALS**
See Sacred Ways; Music &
  Dance

**CHILD
  DEVELOPMENT
  AND LEARNING**
Box of Treasures
Contrary Warriors
Corn Is Life
Hopi
I Know Who I Am
Nomads of the Rain
  Forest
Our Children Are Our
  Future
Robert Davidson
Shenandoah Films (series)
Spirit Bay (series)
Sticks and Stones
Summer of the Loucheux

**CHILDREN,
  PRODUCTIONS
  FOR**
Alaska: The Yup'ik
  Eskimos
Ancient Gift
Apache Mountain Spirits
Celebration
Come Forth Laughing
Corn Is Life

Emergence
Folklore of the Muscogee
  Creek
The Gift of the Sacred
  Dog
Giveaway at Ring
  Thunder
Haudenosaunee
Hopiit
Indian Legends of
  Canada (series)
Lakota Quillwork
Music and Dance of the
  Mohawk
Letter from an Apache
Onenhakenra
Popol Vuh
Spirit Bay (series)
Star Lore
Stickball
A Time to Be Brave
Ute Tribe Video (series)
Walking with
  Grandfather
Whistle in the Wind

**CRAFTS AND
  TECHNIQUES**
Also see Art and Artists;
  Subsistence
An Ancient Gift
Beavertail Snowshoes
Building an Algonkian
  Canoe
Bush Toboggan
By the Work of Our
  Hands
The Craft of Weaving
David Charles
From Hand to Hand
The Earth is Our Home
Ella Mae Blackbear
Indian Hide Tanning
Kleena
KYUK Video (series)
Lakota Quillwork

Maya TV
Music and Dance of the
Mohawk
Nomads of the Rain
Forest
Ojibway and Cree Video
(series)
Our Lives in Our hands
San Pablito Paper
Sticks and Stones
The Traditional Snowshoe
Tule Technology
Traditional Inupiat
Technology (series)

**CULTURE REVIVAL/
SURVIVAL**
Abnaki
Angoon
Box of Treasures
Celebration
Come Forth Laughing
Contrary Warriors
The End of the Race
Eyes of the Spirit
From Hand to Hand
Giveaway at Ring
Thunder
The Great Spirit Within
the Hole
Haa Shagoon
Haudenosaunee
Heart of the Earth
Survival School
Hopi
Huteetl
I Know Who I Am
I'd Rather Be Powwowing
Kaminuriak
Kleena
Lenape
Make Prayers to the
Raven (series)
A Message from Brazil
Mountain Music of Peru
Onenhakenra
Our Lives in Our Hands
Pride, Purpose, Promise
Revival
Robert Davidson
Sacred Circle—Recovery
Seasons of a Navajo
Shenandoah Films (series)
Standing Alone

The Strength of Life
Summer of the Loucheux
Ute Tribe Video (series)
Xochimilco
Yupiit Yuraryarait

CULTURE CHANGE
Abnaki
Alaska: The Yup'ik
Eskimos
Arctic Spirits
Come Forth Laughing
Conversations in
Maranhao
Circle of the Sun
The Craft of Weaving
The End of the Race
Lenape
Guatemala: A Journey
Magic in the Sky
Magic Windows
Onenhakenra
The Pame
The Panare
Sacred Circle—Recovery
Salmon on the Run
San Pablito Paper
Summer of the Loucheux
They Never Asked Our
Fathers
To Put Away the Gods
Todos Santos
Cuchumatan
The Way of the Dead
Indians
A Weave of Time
With the Soul Between
the Teeth
Xunan

ECOLOGY
*See Natural Resources/
Economic Development*

EDUCATION/SCHOOL
Abnaki
Alaska: The Yup'ik
Eskimos
Another Wind Is Moving
Come Forth Laughing
The End of the Race
Faces of Culture (series)
The Great Spirit Within
the Hole

Heart of the Earth
Survival School
Hopi
I Know Who I Am
Inughuit
Maya in Exile
Sacred Circle—Recovery
Shungnak
Through this Darkest
Night
A Weave of Time

ELDERS
Abnaki
Alaska: The Yup'ik
Eskimos
Ancient Spirit, Living
Word
Angoon
Broken Rainbow
By the Work of Our
Hands
Come Forth Laughing
Contrary Warriors
David Charles
The Earth Is Our Home
Eyes of the Spirit
From Hand to Hand
Haa Shagoon
Hopi
Hopiit
Huteetl
Inupiat Legends (series)
Itam Hakim, Hopiit
Kaminuriak
Koyukon Regional
Profiles
Make Prayers to the
Raven (series)
Miken's Way
Ojibway and Cree Video
(series)
Our Sacred Land
The Pipe is the Altar
Seasons of a Navajo
Shenandoah Films (series)
Songs in Minto Life
Standing Alone
Summer of the Loucheux
They Never Asked Our
Fathers
To Put Away the Gods
Traditional Inupiat
Health (series)

: A Journey

  Taytacha
Magic Windows
Make Prayers to the
  Raven (series)
Meta Mayan II
Mexico Indigena (series)
Nomads of the Rain
  Forest
Sacred Circle — Recovery
San Pablito Paper
With the Soul Between
  the Teeth
Xochimilco

MUSIC AND DANCE
Apache Mountain Spirits
Box of Treasures
Celebration
Circle of Song
David Charles
The Drum
The Drum is the Heart
Eyes of the Spirit
Giveaway at Ring
  Thunder
Haa Shagoon
Hikuri Neirra
I'd Rather be Powwowing
In the Footsteps of
  Taytacha
Inughuit
Itam Hakim, Hopiit
The Longest Trail
Mitote Tepehuano
Mountain Music of Peru
Music and Dance of the
  Mohawk
Robert Davidson
Songs in Minto Life
Turtle Shells
The Way of the Dead
  Indians
Yupiit Yuraryarait
Whistle in the Wind

MYTHS AND TALES
Also see Elders; Oral

Traditions
Apache Mountain Spirits
Emergence
The Enchanted Arts
Folklore of the Muscogee
  Creek
The Gift of the Sacred
  Dog
Indian Legends of
  Canada (series)
Inughuit
Inupiat Legends (series)
Itam Hakim, Hopiit
Journey to the Sky
Lakota Quillwork
Onenhakenra
Popol Vuh
Rock Art Treasures
Star Lore
Ute Tribe Video (series)
Walking with
  Grandfather
The Way of the Dead
  Indians

**NATIVE AMERICAN
MEDIA —
CO-PRODUCTIONS**
Abnaki
Apache Mountain Spirits
Box of Treasures
Conversations in
  Maranhao
The Drum is the Heart
Every Day Choices
Haudenosaunee
Huteetl
Koyukon Regional
  Profiles
Jaune Quick-to-See Smith
Make Prayers to the
  Raven (series)
Music and Dance of the
  Mohawks
Onenhakenra
Our Lives in Our Hands
Songs in Minto Life

**NATIVE AMERICAN
INDEPENDENT
MEDIA MAKERS**
Celebration
Eyes of the Spirit

The Great Spirit Within
  the Hole
Heart of the Earth
  Survival School
Hopiit
The Honour of All
I Know Who I Am
I'd Rather Be Powwowing
Itam Hakim, Hopiit
Our Sacred Land
The Pipe Is the Altar
Shenandoah Films (series)
Walking with
  Grandfather
Where We've Been
Yupiit Yuraryariat

**NATIVE AMERICAN
COMMUNITY
MEDIA**
Choctaw Heritage Video
  (series)
Choctaw Video (series)
Come Forth Laughing
Creek Nation Video
  (series)
Kaminuriak
KYUK Video (series)
Magic in the Sky
Northwest Arctic Video
  (series)
Ojibway and Cree Video
  (series)
Ute Tribe Video (series)

**NATURAL
RESOURCES/
ECONOMIC
DEVELOPMENT**
Broken Rainbow
Choctaw Video (series)
The Four Corners
Home of the Brave
Just a Small Fishery
Kaminuriak
Keepers of the Forest
Nomads of the Rain
  Forest
The Panare
The Probable Passing of
  Elk Creek
Pride, Purpose, Promise
Return to Sovereignty
Salmon on the Run

To Put Away the Gods
Xunan

ORAL TRADITIONS/ NATIVE LANGUAGE

See also Elders: Myths and Tales
Abnaki
Ancient Spirit, Living Word
Angoon
Box of Treasures
From Hand to Hand
The Gift of the Sacred Dog
Haa Shagoon
In Our Language
Inughuit
Inupiat Legends (series)
Itam Hakim, Hopiit
KYUK Video (series)
Lenape
Music and Dance of the Mohawk
Northwest Arctic Video (series)
Robert Davidson
Songs in Minto Life
Ute Tribe Video (series)
Xunan

POLITICAL ISSUES

Also see Land; Legislation; Treaties
Abnaki
Angoon
Broken Rainbow
Camino Triste
Contrary Warriors
Conversations in Maranhao
The Four Corners
Guatemala: A Journey
Guatemala: Personal Testimonies
Haa Shagoon
Home of the Brave
Indian Self-Rule
Maya In Exile
A Matter of Trust
A Message from Brazil
Rope to Our Roots

They Never Asked Our Fathers
A Violation of Trust
Voices of Native Americans
When the Mountains Tremble

POWWOWS, FAIRS GIVEAWAYS, AND POTLATCHES

Angoon
Box of Treasures
Celebration
Contrary Warriors
The Drum is the Heart
The Gift of the Sacred Dog
Giveaway at Ring Thunder
Haa Shagoon
Huteetl
I Know Who I Am
I'd Rather Be Powwowing
Make Prayers to the Raven (series)
More than a Week of Fun
The Pame
Songs in Minto Life
Spirit Bay (series)
Standing Alone
Yupiit Yuraryarait

RESERVATION LIFE

Apache Mountain Spirits
Broken Rainbow
Choctaw Video (series)
Contrary Warriors
The Drum Is the Heart
The End of the Race
Giveaway at Ring Thunder
Hopi
I Know Who I Am
Indian Self-Rule
Journey to the Sky
Make My People Live
Onenhakenra
Our Children Are Our Future
Our Sacred Land
Pride, Purpose, Promise
The Probable Passing of Elk Creek

Seasons of a Navajo
Spirit Bay (series)
Standing Alone
Through this Darkest Night
A Weave of Time

SACRED WAYS

Also see Shamanism
Ancient Spirit, Living Word
Apache Mountain Spirits
Arctic Spirits
Corn Is Life
Contrary Warriors
The Drum
Emergence
The End of the Race
The Great Spirit Within the Hole
Green Corn Festival
Haa Shagoon
Haudenosaunee
Hikuri Neirra
Hikuri-Tame
Hopi
Hopiit
Huteetl
I'd Rather Be Powwowing
In the Footsteps of Taytacha
Inughuit
Itam Hakim, Hopiit
Judea
Make Prayers to the Raven (series)
Mara'acame
Maria Sabina
Mexico Indigena (series)
Mitote Tepehuano
Mountain Music of Peru
Music and Dance of the Mohawk
Onenhakenra
Our Sacred Land
The Pame
The Pipe is the Altar
Sacred Circle
Seasons of a Navajo
Shenandoah Films (series)
Standing Alone
Stickball
Teshuinada
To Put Away the Gods

Todos Santos
Cuchumatan
The Way of the Dead
Indians
A Weave of Time
With the Soul Between
the Teeth
Xochimilco

SHAMANISM
Arctic Spirits
Brujos and Healers
Eyes of the Spirit
Hikuri Neirra
Hikuri-Tame
Inughuit
The Longest Trail
Mara'acame
Maria Sabina

**SOVEREIGNTY/
COMMUNITY
CONTROL**
Alaska Native ·Claims
Settlement Act (series)
Angoon
Box of Treasures
Contrary Warriors
Choctaw Video (series)
Home of the Brave
Indian Self-Rule
Magic in the Sky
A Matter of Trust
Pride, Purpose, Promise
The Probable Passing of
Elk Creek
Return to Sovereignty
They Never Asked Our
Fathers
A Violation of Trust
Voices of Native
Americans

**SUBSISTENCE—
FARMING/HERDING**
Alpaca Breeders of
Chimboya
An Ancient Gift
Broken Rainbow
Corn Is Life
Hopi
Hopiit
Keepers of the Forest
Lost in Time

Magic Windows
Nomads of the Rain
Forest
Seasons of a Navajo

**SUBSISTENCE—
HUNTING,
TRAPPING,
FISHING,
GATHERING**
Alaska: The Yup'ik
Eskimos
The Earth Is Our Home
Haa Shagoon
Huteetl
Inughuit
Kaminuriak
Kleena
Lost In Time
Make Prayers to the
Raven (series)
Nomads of the Rain
Forest
The Panare
Salmon on the Run
Shungnak
Songs in Minto Life
Summer of the Loucheux
They Never Asked Our
Fathers
A Time to Be Brave
Traditional Inupiat
Technology (series)
Traditional Migration
Treaty 8 Country
Tule Technology

TREATIES
See Sovereignty; Legislation

**TRIBES AND
REGIONS**
See Tribes and Regions Index

**URBAN LIFE/
RELOCATION**
Broken Rainbow
Contrary Warriors
Doctora
The Great Spirit Within
the Hole
Heart of the Earth
Survival School
Home of the Brave

I'd Rather Be Powwowing
Living Traditions
Make My People Live
Mountain Music of Peru
Our Children Are Our
Future
Pride, Purpose, Promise
The Way of the Dead
Indians
Xochimilco

**WAGE WORK/CASH
ECONOMY**
Alpaca Breeders of
Chimboya
Broken Rainbow
Camino Triste
Choctaw Story
Circle of the Sun
Contrary Warriors
The Craft of Weaving
The End of the Race
Just a Small Fishery
Maya in Exile
Maya TV
Our Lives in Our Hands
The Pame
Pride, Purpose, Promise
Return to Sovereignty
Salmon on the Run
Shungnak
Standing Alone
Todos Santos
Cuchumatan
A Weave of Time
Xochimilco

WOMEN
Abnaki
An Ancient Gift
Ancient Spirit, Living
Word
Arctic Spirits
Box of Treasures
Broken Rainbow
Come Forth Laughing
Contrary Warriors
Corn Is Life
Doctora
The Earth is Our Home
Ella Mae Blackbear
The Enchanted Arts
From Hand to Hand

The Great Spirit Within
 the Hole
Hopi
Huteetl
I Know Who I Am
Jaune Quick-to-See Smith
Kaminuriak
Lakota Quillwork
Living Traditions
Make My People Live
Make Prayers to the
 Raven (series)

Maria Sabina
Onenhakenra
Our Lives in Our Hands
Seasons of a Navajo
Shenandoah Films (series)
Songs in Minto Life
Spirit Bay (series)
Summer of the Loucheux
Through this Darkest
 Night
Todos Santos
 Cuchumatan

Traditional Inupiat
 Healing (series)
Tule Technology
21st Annual World
 Eskimo-Indian
 Olympics
A Weave of Time
When the Mountains
 Tremble
Xunan

TRIBES AND REGIONS

CENTRAL AMERICA: GUATEMALA

Maya
Camino Triste
Faces of Culture (series)
Guatemala: A Journey
Guatemala Personal
Testimonies
Maya In Exile
Meta Mayan II
Popol Vuh
Todos Santos
Cuchumatan
When the Mountains
Tremble

MEXICO
For additional tribes and titles see Mexico Indigena Series

Cora
Judea

Huichol
Hikuri Neirra
Hikuri-Tame
Mara'acame

Maya
Camino Triste
Faces of Culture (series)
Keepers of the Forest
Maya TV
To Put Away the Gods
Xunan

Mazatec
Maria Sabina

Nahua Peoples
Brujos and Healers
(Veracruz)
The Craft of Weaving
(Puebla)
Magic Windows
(Guerrero)

Otomi
San Pablito Paper

Pame
The Pame

Tarahumara
Teshuinada

Tepehuan
Mitote Tepehuano

Totonac
With the Soul Between
the Teeth

Xochimilco
Xochimilco

Zoque-Popoluca
Brujos and Healers
Poetas Campesinos

NORTH AMERICA AND THE ARCTIC

Alabama and Coushatta
Journey to the Sky

Anishinabe
See Ojibwa

Apache
Apache Mountain Spirits
(White Mountain)
Letter from an Apache
(Chiricahua)

Athapaskan Groups
(Alaska and Canada)
*See Beaver, Dené Thá,
Koyukon, Kutchin,
Tanana*

Beaver
Treaty 8 Country

Blackfoot Confederacy
Circle of the Sun
The Drum is the Heart

Sacred Circle
Sacred Circle — Recovery
Standing Alone

Blood
See Blackfoot Confederacy

California Tribes
*Also see Grinding Rock
Band, Pomo, Yurok*
Rock Art Treasures
Shenandoah Films (series)

Choctaw
Choctaw Video (series)

Cherokee
Ella Mae Blackbear
The Strength of Life

Cheyenne
In Our Language
Our Sacred Land

Chippewa
See Ojibwa

Cree
Indian Legends of
Canada (series)
Ojibway and Cree Video
(series)
Trust for Native American
Cultures & Crafts
(series)

Creek
Creek Nation Video
(series)
Green Corn Festival
Make My People Live
The Strength of Life

Crow
Contrary Warriors
The Gift of the Sacred
Dog

Delaware
See Lenape

Dené Thá
Sacred Circle — Recovery

Eskimo
See Inuit/Eskimo

Flathead
Indian Self-Rule

Gitskan
Revival

Grinding Rock Band
The Probable Passing of
 Elk Creek

Gros Ventre
I'd Rather Be Powwowing

Haida
Revival
Robert Davidson

Hopi
Corn is Life
The Four Corners
Hopi: Songs of the
 Fourth World
Hopiit
Itam Hakim, Hopiit

Inuit/Eskimo (*Canada*)
Animations at Cape
 Dorset
Arctic Spirits
Kaminuriak
Magic in the Sky
Rope to Our Roots
Siksilarmiut

Inuit/Eskimo
 (*Greenland*)
Inughuit
Rope to Our Roots

Inuit/Eskimo: Inupiat
 (*Alaska*)
Inupiat Eskimo Healing
Northwest Arctic Video
 (series)
Rope to Our Roots
Shungnak
21st Annual World
 Eskimo-Indian
 Olympics

Inuit/Eskimo: Yup'ik
 (*Alaska*)
Alaska: The Yup'ik

Eskimos
Every Day Choices
Eyes of the Spirit
From Hand to Hand
KYUK Video (series)
A Matter of Trust
Rope to Our Roots
They Never Asked Our
 Fathers
21st Annual World
 Eskimo-Indian
 Olympics
Yupiit Yuraryariat

Iroquois Confederacy
See Mohawk, Onondaga

Kainai (Blood)
See Blackfoot Confederacy

Kickapoo
Return to Sovereignty

Koyukon
Huteetl
Koyukon Regional
 Profiles
Make Prayers to the
 Raven (series)

Kutchin
Summer of the Loucheux

Kwakiutl
Box of Treasures
Kleena

Lakota
See Sioux Nations

Lenape
Lenape

Loucheux
See Kutchin

Makah
I Know Who I Am

Malecite
Abnaki

Mashpee Wampanoag
Mashpee

Micmac
Abnaki
Indian Legends of
 Canada (series)
Our Lives in Our Hands

Mohawk
The Drum
Haudenosaunee
Music and Dance of the
 Mohawk
Onenhakenra

Navajo
An Ancient Gift
Broken Rainbow
Emergence
The Four Corners
Home of the Brave
Indian Self-Rule
Make My People Live
Seasons of a Navajo
A Weave of Time

Nishga
Revival

Nisqually
I Know Who I Am

Ojibwa (*Canada and US*)
Celebration
Heart of the Earth
 Survival School
Indian Legends of
 Canada (series)
Living Traditions
Ojibway and Cree Video
 (series)
Spirit Bay (series)
Trust for Native American
 Cultures & Crafts
 (series)

Onondaga
Haudenosaunee

Pomo
The Path of Our Elders

Paiute
The Earth is Our Home
Pride, Purpose, Promise
Tule Technology

Passamaquoddy
Abnaki

Penobscot
Abnaki

Pueblos (*Eastern*)
The Enchanted Arts
The End of the Race

Puyallup
I Know Who I Am

Quinault
Indian Self-Rule

Sioux Nations
The Pipe is the Altar (see
  Celebration)
Giveaway at Ring
  Thunder
Home of the Brave
Lakota Quillwork
Living Traditions
Make My People Live
Our Sacred Land

Slave
See Dené Thá

Suquamish
Come Forth Laughing

Tanana
Songs in Minto Life

Tlingit
Angoon

Haa Shagoon
Make My People Live

Ute
Ute Tribe Video (series)

Yavapai
Letter from an Apache

Yurok
Our Songs Will Never
  Die
Salmon on the Run

SOUTH AMERICA

Aymara and Quechua
  (Bolivia)
Aymara Leadership
Doctora
Faces of Culture (series)
Home of the Brave

Aymara and Quechua
  (Peru)
Alpaca Breeders of
  Chimboya
Choqela

In the Footsteps of
  Taytacha
Mountain Music of Peru
Whistle in the Wind

Canela-Apanyekra
  (Brazil)
Conversations in
  Maranhao

Guajiro (Venezuela/
  Columbia)
The Way of the Dead
  Indians

Kraho (Brazil)
A Message from Brazil

Panare (Venezuela)
The Panare

Shuar/Lowland Quichua
  (Ecuador)
Home of the Brave

Waorani (Ecuador)
Nomads of the Rain
  Forest

DISTRIBUTORS
Volume I and Volume II

ADL/Anti-Defamation League of B'nai Brith. 823 United Nations Plaza, New York, NY 10017. Attn: Steve Brody. (212) 490-2525.

Agnello Films. 31 Maple St., Ridgefield Park, NJ 07660. (201) 807-0662.

AIMS Media. 6901 Woodley Ave., Van Nuys, CA 91406. (800) 367-2467.

Akwesasne Museum. Route 37, Hogansburg, NY 13655. (518) 358-2240.

American Indian Treaty Council. The distributor is Upstream Productions.

ANFP. The distributor is Camera One.

Assoc. Films. The distributor is Karol Media.

Auburn Television. Auburn University, Auburn, AL 36849. (205) 826-4110.

Aurora Films. P. O. Box 020164, Juneau, AK 99802-0164. (907) 586-6696.

B&C Films. Rental distributors are MICH and UCEMC.

Barr Films. P. O. Box 7878, Irwindale, CA 91706-7878. (800) 234-7878.

Beacon Films. P. O. Box 575, Norwood, MA 02062. (617) 762-0811.

Beecher. For distribution information contact: Promotion Dept., KUTV-TV, P. O. Box 30901, Salt Lake City, UT 84301. Attn: Maria Smith. (801) 973-3375.

BFA. See Phoenix/BFA.

Billip-Harris. 626 E. 20th St., 3A, New York, NY 10003. (212) 982-7131.

Blackhawk. Box 3990, 1235 W. Fifth St., Davenport, IA 52808. (319) 323-9736.

Boreal Institute for Northern Studies Library, University of Alberta. CW-401 Biological Sciences Bldg., Edmonton, Alberta, Canada T6G 2E9. (403) 432-4409.

Bosustow. Distributors are Churchill Films and PSU.

Bo Boudart Films. 2079 Edgewood Dr., Palo Alto, CA 94303. (415) 856-2004.

Bowling Green. The distributor is Jack Ofield Productions, P. O. Box 12792, San Diego, CA 92112. (619) 462-8266.

Margaret Brandon. 140 Ridgeway Rd., Woodside, CA 94062. (415) 369-0139.

Brown. The distributor is IFB.

Buffalo Bill Historical Center, Education Dept. Box 1000, Cody, WY 82414. (307) 587-4771.

Bullfrog Films, Oley, PA 19547. US: (800) 543-3764. In PA: (215) 779-8226.

BYU/Brigham Young University, Educational Media Center. 101 Fletcher Bldg., Provo, UT 84602. (801) 378-2713.

BYU/NAS. For information contact FVC-MAI.

CA. The distributor of MORE THAN BOWS AND ARROWS is Camera One. The distributor of IMAGES OF INDIANS is PLP.

Dave Caldwell Productions. 26934 Halifax Pl., Hayward, CA 94542. (415) 538-4286.

Camera One Productions. 431-A North 34th St., Seattle, WA 98103. (206) 547-5131.

Canadian Learning Co. 2229 Kingston Rd., Suite 203, Scarborough, Ontario, Canada M1N 1T8. (416) 265-3333.

Arthur Cantor Films. 2112 Broadway, Suite 400, New York, NY 10023. (212) 496-5710.

Canyon Cinema. 2325 3rd St., Suite 338, San Francisco, CA 94107. (415) 626-2255.

CAR. For information contact FVC-MAI.

Catticus Corporation. 2600 10th St., Berkeley, CA 94710. (415) 548-0854.

Centre Productions. 1800 30th St., Suite 207, Boulder, CO 80301. US: (800) 824-1166. In CO: (303) 444-1166.

Centro de Produccion de Cortometraje. Estudios Churueusco, Atletas #2, Mexico, D. F., Mexico.

CFMDC. The distributor is CFDW.

CFDW/Canadian Filmmakers Distribution West. 1131 Howe St., Suite 100, Vancouver, British Columbia, Canada V6Z 2L7. (604) 684-3014.

Chevron. Videotape: Community Affairs, Chevron USA. 575 Market St., San Francisco, CA 94105. Attn: Carrie Murphy. (415) 894-5193. Study guide: Chevron USA. 742 Bancroft Way, Berkeley, CA 94710.

Choctaw Heritage Video. Route 7, Box 21, Philadelphia, MS 39350. (601) 656-5251.

Choctaw Video Productions. Route 7, Box 21, Philadelphia, MS 39350. (601) 656-5251.

Churchill Films. 662 N. Robertson Blvd., Los Angeles, CA 90069. (213) 657-5110.

CICH/Canadian Institute of Child Health. 17 York St., Ottawa, Ontario, Canada K1N 5S7. (613) 238-8425.

CIMA. 52 E. 1st St., New York, NY 10003. (212) 673-1666.

The Cinema Guild. 1697 Broadway, Suite 802, New York, NY 10019. (212) 246-5522.

CLC/Canadian Learning Co., Inc. 2229 Kingston Rd., Scarborough, Ontario, Canada M1N 1T8. (416) 265-3333.

Clearwater Publishing. The distributor is Norman Ross Publishing.

Coast Telecourses. 11460 Warner Ave., Fountain Valley, CA 92708. (714) 241-6109.

Cohen. The distributor of John Cohen's films is The Cinema Guild.

COR/Coronet-MTI Films and Video. 108 Wilmot Rd., Deerfield, IL 60015. US: (800) 621-2131. In AK, IL: (312) 940-1260.

C-S. The distributor of Juan Downey's videotapes is EAI.

DA. The distributor is The Cinema Guild.

Denver Art Museum, Education Dept. 100 W. 14th Ave. Pkwy., Denver, CO 80204. (303) 575-2312.

Irene-Aimee Depke. 5627 N. Neva Ave., Chicago, IL 60631. (312) 642-1234.

DER/Documentary Educational Resources. 101 Morse St., Watertown, MA 02172. (617) 926-0491. All Odyssey programs are distributed on film by DER and on video by PBS Video.

Direct Cinema Limited. P. O. Box 69589, Los Angeles, CA 90069. (213) 652-8000.

Direction Films. 92 Scarborough Rd., Toronto, Ontario, Canada M4E 3M5. (416) 698-6237.

DTC-TV/Downtown Community Television. 87 Lafayette St., New York, NY 10013. (212) 966-4510.

EAI/Electronic Arts Intermix. 10 Waverly Pl., New York, NY 10003. (212) 473-6822.

Earthworm. The distributors are Flower Films and UTFL.

EBE/Encyclopedia Brittanica. 425 N. Michigan Ave., Chicago, IL 60611. (312) 347-7000.

Nicolas Echevarria. Calle San Jeronimo 5, Casa 3, Colonia San Jeronimo Lidice, Mexico, D. F. 10200, Mexico.

EDC/Educational Development Center. 55 Chapel St., Newton, MA 02158. (617) 969-7100. For information about CESAR'S BARK CANOE contact FVC-MAI.

Educational Media. For information contact FVC-MAI.

Em Gee Film Library. 6924 Canby, #103, Reseda, CA 91335. (818) 981-5506.

Wayne Ewing, Box 32269, Washington, D.C. 20007. (202) 328-0955.

FACSEA/French-American Cultural Services and Educational Aid. 972 Fifth Ave., New York, NY 10021. (212) 582-8870.

FC. A rental distributor is UUT.

FCE. Distributors include Blackhawk, Em Gee, and UUT.

Ferrero Films. 1259-A Folsom St., San

Francisco, CA 94102. (415) 626-3456.

FFC/Film Fair Communcations. 10900 Ventura Blvd., P. O. Box 1728, Studio City, CA 91604. (818) 985-0244.

FH/Films for the Humanities. P. O. Box 2053, Princeton, NJ 08543. US: (800) 257-5126. In AK, HI, NJ: (609) 452-1128.

FI/Films Incorporated-PMI. 5547 N. Ravenswood Ave., Chicago, IL 60640-1199. US: (800) 323-4222. In IL: (312) 878-2600 or 878-7300. The distributor of Q'EROS is The Cinema Guild. For information about HOPI WAY, NAVAJO WAY, and TUKTU STORIES contact FVC-MAI.

Film in the Cities. 2388 University Ave., Minneapolis, MN 55114. (612) 646-6104.

Film Wright. 4530 18th St., San Francisco, CA 94114. (415) 863-6100.

Flower Films. 10341 San Pablo Ave., El Cerrito, CA 94530. (415) 525-0942.

Four Worlds Development Project. Faculty of Education, The University of Lethbridge. 4401 University Dr., Lethbridge, Alberta, Canada T1K 3M4. Attn: Cheryl Ackroyd. (403) 329-2435.

Full Circle Communications. 1131 South College, Tulsa, OK 74104.

Fulton Films. 64 Orchard Hill Rd., Newton, CT 06070. (203) 426-2580.

FVC-MAI/Film and Video Center, Museum of the American Indian. Broadway at 155th St., New York, NY 10032. (212) 283-2420.

Chris Gaul. 1919 Old Turkey Point Rd., Baltimore, MD 21211. (301) 686-7273.

GPN/Great Plains National. P. O. Box 80669, Lincoln, NE 68501. US: (800) 228-4630. In HI, NE: (402) 472-2007.

Granada Television International. 35 Golden Square, London, England W1R 4AH.

Green Mountain Cine Works. 53 Hamilton Ave., Staten Island, NY 10301. Attn: Nick Manning. (718) 981-0120.

Edgar Heap of Birds. Route 1, Box 89B, Cheyenne-Arapaho Nation, Geary, OK 73040. (405) 884-2741.

Brian Huberman. c/o Rice University Media Center, P. O. Box 1892, Houston, TX 77251. (713) 527-4882.

Hugaitha. The distributor is UCLA-IML.

IASU/Iowa State University, Media Resource Center. 121 Pearson Hall, Ames, IA 50011. (515) 294-1540.

IBC/Inuit Broadcasting Corporation. 251 Laurier Ave. West, Suite 703, Ottawa, Ontario, Canada K1P 5J6. (613) 235-1892.

Icarus Films. 200 Park Ave. South, Room 1319, New York, NY 10003. (212) 674-3375.

Idemedia. The distributor is Interama, 301 W. 53rd St., Suite 19E, New York, NY 10019. (212) 977-4830.

IDIL/Institute for the Development of Indian Law. 1104 Glyndon St. SE, Vienna, VA 22180. (703) 938-7822.

IFB/International Film Bureau. 322 So. Michigan Ave., Chicago, IL 60604. (312) 427-4545.

IFF/International Film Foundation. 155 W. 72nd St., New York, NY 10023. (212) 580-1111.

Image Film. 132 Hampshire Dr., Rochester, NY 14618. (716) 473-8070.

INI/Instituto Nacional Indigenista. Archivo Etnografico Audio-visual, Av. Revolucion 1227, 4 piso, Mexico D.F., Mexico. Attn: Dr. Eduardo Ahued.

Investigative Productions. 48 Major St., Toronto, Ontario, Canada M5S 2L1. (416) 968-7818.

Intermedia Arts Minnesota. 425 Ontario St. SE, Minneapolis, MN 55414. (416) 627-4444.

IS Productions. P. O. Box 747, Hotevilla, AZ 86030.

ISHI. The rental distributor for Granada films is THA.

ITFE/International Tele-Film Enterprises. 47 Densley Ave., Toronto, Ontario, Canada M6M 5A8. (416) 241-4483.

IU/Indiana University Audio Visual Center. Bloomington, IN 47405. (812) 335-2103.

Johnston Films. 16 Valley Rd., Princeton, NJ 08540. (609) 924-7505.

Karol Media. 22 Riverview Dr., Wayne, NJ 07470. (201) 628-9111.

Margrit Keller. Predigerplatz 44, CH-8001 Zurich, Switzerland.

KUAC-TV, University of Alaska-Fairbanks. Fairbanks, AK 99775. (907) 474-7492.

KUHT-TV. 4513 Cullen Blvd., Houston, TX 77004. Attn: Steve Pyndus. (713) 749-7371.

KUSD-TV. 414 E. Clark St., Vermillion, SD 57069. Attn: Shirley Sneve, Minority Affairs Programs. (605) 677-5861.

KYUK Video Productions. Pouch 468, Bethel, AK 99559. (907) 543-3131.

Donna and Bill Land. 2301 W. Las Lomitas, Tucson, AZ. (602) 293-3111.

LCA. The distributor is COR.

Norman Lippman. 7745 Mohawk Pl., St. Louis, MO 63105 (314) 725-3313.

Lodestar Films. 42-28 E. 103rd St., Tulsa, OK 74136. (918) 299-6717.

Lost Nation Films. 1012 Timber Trail, Dixon, Il 61021. (815) 652-4754.

Lucerne Media. 37 Ground Pine Rd., Morris Plains, NJ 07950. US: (800) 341-2293. In NJ: (201) 538-1401.

Verity Lund. 173 Avenue C, New York, NY 10009. (212) 505-5712.

MAC. The distributor of I WILL FIGHT NO MORE FOREVER and MAYA-LAND is FI. For information about DRY WEATHER CHRONICLE contact FVC-MAI.

Magic Lantern. The distributor is Alexander Milenic, 8506 Salem Way, Bethesda, MD 20814. (301) 657-3232.

MLFD. Magic Lantern Film Distributors, Ltd. 136 Cross Ave., Oakville, Ontario, Canada L6J 2W6. (416) 844-7216.

Matrix Video Services. #10-2425 Granville St., Vancouver, British Columbia, Canada V6H 3G5. (604) 261-3886.

McCarthy. The distributor is OneWest Media.

Maureen McNamara. 12 Vincent St., Cambridge, MA 02140. (617) 661-0402.

MCNCC/Muscogee Creek Nation Communication Center. P. O. Box 580, Okmulgee, OK 74447. (918) 756-8700.

Media Guild. 11562 Sorrento Valley Rd., Suite J, San Diego, CA 92121. (619) 755-9191.

MGS. The distributor is UCEMC.

MICH/Michigan Media. 400 Fourth St., Ann Arbor, MI 48103-4816. (313) 764-5360.

MOMA/Museum of Modern Art. 11 W. 53rd St., New York, NY 10019. (212) 708-9530.

MP/The Media Project. P. O. Box 2008, Portland, OR 97208. (503) 223-5335.

NAPBC/Native American Public Broadcasting Consortium. P. O. Box 83111, Lincoln, NE 68501. (402) 472-3522.

NAVC/National AudioVisual Center. 8700 Edgeworth Dr., Capitol Heights, MD 20743. (202) 763-1896.

NETCHE is now named NETV.

NETV/Nebraska Educational Television. P. O. Box 83111, Lincoln, NE 68501. Attn: Steve Lenzen. US: (800) 228-4630. In HI, NE: (402) 472-2007.

The Newark Museum. 49 Washington St., Newark, NJ 07101. (201) 733-6600.

New Day Films. Bookings: 22 Riverview Dr., Wayne, NJ 07470-3191, (201) 633-0212. Information: 853 Broadway, Suite 1210, New York, NY 10003. (212) 477-4604.

New Yorker Films. 16 W. 61st St., New York, NY 10023. (212) 247-6110.

NFBC/National Film Board of Canada. 1251 Avenue of the Americas, 16th floor, New York, NY 10020. (212) 586-5131.

Norman Ross Publishing (sales only). Rentals available on ½" vt from ATLATL, 402 W. Roosevelt, Phoenix, AZ 85003. (602) 253-2731.

North American Indian Films. The distributor of NORTH AMERICAN INDIAN ARTS AND CRAFTS SERIES is ITFE. The distributor of NOUISE KENE is CICH.

Northern Heritage Films. P. O. Box 82007, Fairbanks, AK 99708. (907) 479-5253.

Northwest Arctic Television Center. P. O. Box 51, Kotzebue, AK 99752. Attn: Bob Walker. (907) 442-3672.

ODE/Oklahoma Department of Education, Media Resources, Oliver Hodge Building, Oklahoma City, OK 73105.

Ojibway and Cree Cultural Centre. 84 Elm South, Timmins, Ontario, Canada P4N 1W6. (705) 267-7911.

OneWest Media. 535 Cordova Rd., Suite 410, Santa Fe, NM 87501. (505) 983-8685.

OPB/Oregon Public Broadcasting. 2828 SW Front Ave., Portland, OR 97201. (503) 295-2412.

Pacific Cinematheque. The distributor of POTLATCH is CFDW. For information about THE LAND IS THE CULTURE contact Susan Ross, Pacific Cinematheque. (604) 688-8202.

Pacific International Enterprises. 1133 S. Riverside, Suite #1, Medford, OR 97501. (503) 779-0990.

PBS Video. 1320 Braddock Pl., Alexandria, VA 22314-1698. Information: (800) 424-7964. Orders: (800) 344-3337. For information about CONCERNS OF AMERICAN INDIAN WOMEN and THIEVES OF TIME contact FVC-MAI.

Phoenix-BFA Films and Video. 468 Park Ave. South, New York, NY 10016. (212) 684-5910.

PI. For information contact Boudart.

PLP/Phil Lucas Productions. P.O. Box 1218, Issaquah, WA 98027. (206) 392-9482.

Linda Post-Eugene Rosow. 434 Sycamore Rd., Santa Monica, CA 90402. (213) 459-9448.

Preloran. The distributor is UCEMC.

PSU/The Pennsylvania State University Audio Visual Services. University Park, PA 16802. (814) 865-6314.

Pyramid Film and Video. Box 1048, Santa Monica, CA 90406-1048. (800) 421-2304.

Ritz. The distributor is Brown Bird Productions, 1971 N. Curson Ave., Hollywood, CA 09946. (213) 851-8928.

Rodgers. The distributor is Gail Singer Films, 82 Willcocks St., Toronto, Ontario, Canada M5S 1C8. (416) 923-4245.

San Juan School District Media Center. Curriculum Division, Box 804, Blanding, UT 84511. (801) 678-2281.

Alan Saperstein. 1425 N.W. 25th Terrace, Gainesville, FL 32605. (904) 377-5392.

The Saul Zaentz Production Co. 2600 10th St., Berkeley, CA 94710. (800) 227-0602.

SCET/Southwest Center for Educational Televisiion. 7703 N. Lamar Blvd., Suite 500, Austin, TX 78752. Attn: Frederick Close. (512) 454-6811.

Seneca Nation. The distributor is the Seneca-Iroquois National Museum. P. O. Box 442, Salamanca, NY 14779. (716) 945-1738.

Serious Business. Distributors of EDUARDO THE HEALER include PSU and UCEMC. The distributor of THE BELL THAT RANG TO AN EMPTY SKY is Canyon.

SFL. Rental distributors include UAZ.

Shenandoah Film Productions, 538 G. St., Arcata, CA 95521. (707) 822-1030.

Silvercloud Video Productions, 1321 E. King Rd., Tucson, AZ 85719. (602) 326-7647.

Smith. The distributor of THE MAYA OF CONTEMPORARY YUCATAN (now titled THE LIVING MAYA) is UCEMC. AYMARA LEADERSHIP is distributed by Hubert Smith, P. O. Box 150, Selma, OR 97538. (503) 597-2142.

Solaris. 264 W. 19th St., New York, NY 10011. (212) 741-0778.

Spotted Eagle Productions. 2524 Hennepin Ave. South, Minneapolis, MN 55405. (612) 377-4212.

Sterling Educational Films. 711 Fifth Ave., New York, NY 10022. (212) 759-5727.

George C. Stoney. Dept. of Film/TV, New York University, TSOA, 721 Broadway, #944, New York, NY 10014.

Claude Stresser-Pean. Hegel 703-502, Mexico, D.F., 11580 Mexico.

Suquamish Museum. P.O. Box 498, Suquamish, WA 98392. (206) 598-3311.

Synapse. The distributor of THE ABANDONED SHIBONO is EAI. The distributor of COMISARIO FAUSTINO is Billip-Harris. The distributor of THIS SIDE (full title — THIS SIDE OF THE RIVER) is Wali.

Tamarack Films. 11032-76 St., Edmonton, Alberta, Canada T5B 2C6. (403) 477-7958.

Texture Films. The distributor is FI.

THA/Thomas Howe Associates Ltd. 1226 Homer St., Suite 1, Vancouver, British Columbia, Canada V6B 2Y8. (604) 687-4215.

THRC/Texas Humanities Resource Center. 1600 Nueces, Austin, TX 78701. (512) 482-0883.

TLV/Time-Life Video. 100 Eisenhower Dr., Paramus, NJ 07652. (800) 526-4663. Rental distributors of MYSTERY OF THE ANASAZI include IASU, PSU, and UMN.

Andrea Tonacci. Rua Conselheiro Brotero, 1559, Apto. 134, Sao Paulo 01232, Brazil.

The Trust for Native American Cultures and Crafts. Box 142, Greenville, NH 03048. (603) 878-2944.

Tulalip Tribe Fisheries. 3901 Totem Beach Rd., Marysville, WA 98270. Attn: Daryl Williams. (206) 653-0220.

TWN/Third World Newsreel. 335 W. 38th St. 5th Floor, New York, NY 10018. (212) 947-9277.

UAL/Department of Radio and Television, University of Alberta. Edmonton, Alberta, Canada T6G 2E9. (403) 432-4962.

UAZ/University of Arizona Film Library. Audio-Visual Bldg., Tucson, AZ 85721. (602) 621-3282. The distributor of HO-

HOKAM is Land.

UCEMC/University of California Extension Media Center. 2176 Shattuck Ave., Berkeley, CA 94704. (415) 642-0462.

UCLA-IML/Instructional Media Library, University of California at Los Angeles. Royce Hall, Room 8, Los Angeles, CA 90024. (213) 825-0755.

UEVA. The distributor is THA.

UFSI/Universities Field Staff International. 620 Union Dr., Indianapolis, IN 46202. (317) 264-4122.

UIL/University of Illinois Film Center. 1325 South Oak St., Champaign, IL 61820. US: (800) 367-3456. In IL: (800) 252-1357.

UKS. The distributor of NESHNABEK is UCEMC.

UMC/Utah Media Arts Center. 20 South West Temple, Salt Lake City, UT 84101. (801) 534-1158.

UMid. The distributor is GPN.

UMN/University of Minnesota Film and Video. 1313 Fifth St. S.E., Minneapolis, MN 55414. US: (800) 847-8251. In MN: (612) 373-3810.

UNI. Titles now distributed by The Cinema Guild are: BROKEN TREATY AT BATTLE MOUNTAIN, COST OF COTTON, COURAGE OF THE PEOPLE, CROW DOG, I SPENT MY LIFE IN THE MINES, and LISTEN CARACAS. Titles now distributed by New Yorker Films are: BLOOD OF THE CONDOR and CHUQIAGO.

UNV/University of Nevada Film Library. Getchell Library, Reno, NV 89557. (702) 784-6037.

Upstream Productions. 420 First Ave. West, Studio B, Seattle, WA 98119. (206) 281-9177.

Ute Indian Tribe Audio-Visual. P. O. Box 129, Fort Duchesne, UT 84026. Attn: Larry Cesspooch. (801) 722-5141.

UTFL/University of Texas Film Library, Drawer W, Austin, TX 78711. (512) 471-3573.

UUT/University of Utah, Instructional Media Center. 207 Milton Bennion Hall, Salt Lake City, UT 84112. (801) 581-3170.

UWA/University of Washington, Instructional Media Services. 23 Kane Hall, DG-10, Seattle, WA 98195. (206) 543-9909.

VOI/Video Out International. 1160 Hamilton St., Vancouver, British Columbia, Canada V6B 2S2. (604) 688-4336.

WA. For information contact FVC-MAI.

Wallace. The distributor is Lucerne.

Monona Wali. 886 S. Bronson Ave., Los Angeles, CA 90005. (213) 650-7341.

Wenner-Gren. For information contact FVC-MAI.

WGBH. The distributor of FEATHERS is GPN. A rental distributor of THE LONG WALK OF FRED YOUNG is UMN. For information on UMEALIT contact FVC-MAI.

Wheelock. The distributor is UFSI.

WNET-13 Video Distribution. 356 W. 58th St., New York, NY 10019. (212) 560-3045.

The Works. 1659 18th St., Santa Monica, CA 90404. (213) 828-8643.

WXXI-TV. For information contact FVC-MAI.

Zia Cine. P. O. Box 493, Santa Fe, NM 87504. (505) 983-4127.

FILM AND VIDEO CENTER

The Film and Video Center of the Museum of the American Indian provides information about and exhibits films and videotapes concerned with Inuit and Indian peoples of North, Central, and South America. Its on-going activities include:

NATIVE AMERICAN FILM AND VIDEO FESTIVAL and PROGRAMMING SERVICES

The Center exhibits the work of independent film- and videomakers and Native American media centers. Its nationally-recognized Native American Film and Video Festival, in New York City, and its national traveling festivals showcase outstanding new productions. The Center also prepares exhibitions for host institutions and offers programming assistance.

INFORMATION SERVICES and CONSULTANCIES

The Center provides information to the public about archival and recent films and videotapes and has published two volumes of the catalog NATIVE AMERICANS ON FILM AND VIDEO. It assists media makers with information on exhibition, distribution, and funding, and has organized symposia on issues in Native American media and workshops in production skills. Consultancies and footage research are available to programmers and media producers.

FILM AND VIDEO STUDY COLLECTION/ARCHIVES

A study collection of archival and recent works is available for viewing at the Film and Video Center. It includes films made before 1930, films produced by Canada's National Film Board and Mexico's Instituto Nacional Indigenista, and works by award-winning independent film- and videomakers and Native American media groups.

CALL FOR INFORMATION AND DONATIONS TO THE COLLECTION:

The Film and Video Center is currently soliciting information about all films and videotapes on Native Americans to include in a comprehensive database to supplement the published information on NATIVE AMERICANS ON FILM AND VIDEO. Persons with information about archival and recent works to be listed in the database, or who wish to donate or lend works to the study collection, are urged to contact the staff of the Film and Video Center, Museum of the American Indian, Broadway at 155th Street, New York, NY 10032, (212) 283-2420.